FOLK-LORE OF WOMEN

FOLK-LORE OF WOMEN

AS

ILLUSTRATED BY LEGENDARY AND TRADITIONARY TALES, FOLK-RHYMES, PROVERBIAL SAYINGS, SUPERSTITIONS, ETC.

BY

T. F. THISELTON-DYER, M.A. OXON

TYNRON PRESS
DUMFRIESSHIRE

First published in 1905

This edition published in 1990 by
Tynron Press
Stenhouse
Thornhill
Dumfriesshire DG3 4LD
Scotland

ISBN 1-871948-37-1

Cover design by John Hall
Printed in Singapore by Fong & Sons Printers Pte. Ltd.

PREFACE

IN one of his essays, Emerson tells us that "proverbs, like the sacred books of each nation, are the sanctuary of the intuitions," a statement which, if accepted, must place this class of literature on a very high footing. But, although due caution must be taken, when analysing proverbial lore, to differentiate between the serious and jocular element contained therein, it may safely be said that, taken as a whole, such adages and saws—which form an important branch of folk-lore—express more or less correctly the estimate of mankind relative to the subject specially handled. And, when it is remembered what a wealth of material proverbial literature supplies in connection with every concern of daily life, it is not surprising that woman should have been made a prominent theme for criticism and comment, the judgment passed on her being in most cases fairly evenly divided between what is in her favour or the reverse.

In a field, too, so wide we have been content to cull, from here and there, sufficient typical instances of the proverbial wisdom of the human race in its teaching of woman's character as to illustrate the subjects classified in the following chapters, without unduly multiplying examples, which only too frequently are a repetition of the same adage told in a different form.

And, although at one time or another numerous volumes have been published on woman, no work similar to the present one has been attempted in this country, wherein we have endeavoured in a handy and concise form to classify under their subjective headings the proverbial sayings, folk-rhymes, superstitions, and traditionary lore associated with the fair sex. Some years ago, however, a valuable and interesting work was issued in Paris by Pierre Marie Quitard, entitled "Proverbes sur les femmes, l'amitié l'amour, &c.," which contains much curious information, and the introductory chapter of Kelly's useful volume, "Proverbs of all Nations, Compared, Explained, and Illustrated," is devoted to women, love, and marriage. Among some of the works published in England on proverbial literature to which we are indebted are Christy's "Proverbs of All Ages" (2 vols., 1888), Denny's "Proverbs of Many Nations," William Stirling's "Essay towards a Collection of Books relating to Proverbs, &c." (1860), H. H. Vaughan's "Welsh Proverbs," Hislop's "Proverbs of Scotland" (1870), Macintosh's "Gaelic Proverbs" (1882), and Standing's "Anecdotes and Proverbs" (1891), besides the various works issued by the Folk-Lore Society, the several series of *Notes and Queries*—to the pages of which folk-lorists owe a deep debt of gratitude, information chronicled therein not to be found elsewhere—and a recent useful work on "Proverb Lore," by F. E. Hulme.

Among older works which deserve perusal may be noticed John Heywood's "Dialogue and Epigrams," which made its first appearance in 1546, and the famous work of John Ray, which was issued in 1670, and was incorporated by Mr. Bohn in his "Handbook of Proverbs," published in 1857. Herbert's "Outlandish Proverbs," printed in 1640, contains many curious and amusing sayings, and one section of Camden's "Remains," which first appeared in 1605, is devoted to a collection of proverbs.

Mr. Hazlitt, in his preface to his "English Proverbs and Proverbial Phrases" (1869), has made a valuable survey of the literature of proverb-lore in this country, and Dean Trench, in his introduction to his "Proverbs and their Lessons," alluding to "the immense number and variety of books bearing on the subject," truly remarks that most of these compilations "include matter which cannot fitly be placed before all, or they address themselves to the scholar alone ; or, if not so, are at any rate inaccessible to the mere English reader ; or they contain bare lists of proverbs, with no endeavour to compare, illustrate, or explain them—or, if they do seek to explain, they yet do it without attempting to sound the depths or measure the real significance of that which they attempt to unfold." For the same reason we have been obliged to omit a very large number of proverbs as unsuitable for the general reader, although, unfortunately, very many of these old adages are witty and amusing, but their coarseness renders them out of place in a work of the present kind.

Many valuable works illustrative of foreign proverb-lore have appeared at intervals, and, in addition to those connected with France already quoted, may be noticed "Les Proverbes de la langue française," par D. Loubens (1889), A. Mariette's "French and English Proverbs" (1896–7), G. Belcour's "Selection of French Proverbs," and M. de Lincy's "French Collection of Proverbs," published in two volumes in 1880.

Much that is interesting in connection with womankind will be found in J. Barten's "Collection of English and German Proverbs" (1890), and in J. Muddlemore's "Proverbs in Various Languages" (1889); and an old work which deserves notice is Torriano's "Italian Proverbs," published as far back as 1666. It may be added that a large number of publications on proverb-lore which illustrate our subject have been published abroad, many of which, although not easily accessible elsewhere, may be seen at the British Museum; and amongst some of the works to which we are indebted may be mentioned J. R. Jewett's "Arabic Proverbs" (1891), being the fifteenth volume of the American Oriental Society, S. W. Fallon's "Hindustani Proverbs" (1880), P. R. T. Gurdon's "Assamese Proverbs" (1896), G. Bayan's "Armenian Proverbs" (1889), and an interesting little volume on "Kashmiri Proverbs," by J. H. Knowles, which was published at Bombay in 1885.

In 1890 there was issued at Colombo a good collection of Sinhalese and European proverbs by N. Mendis, and in 1897 Mr. H. Jensen produced his "Tamil Proverbs," which contains much that has its counterpart in our own proverbial lore relating to woman; while Mr. W. F. Johnson's "Hindi Proverbs" (1886) further largely adds to the estimate formed of the fair sex.

Mr. A. H. Smith's "Chinese Proverbs" is excellent as far as it goes, and Mr. Pfoundes, in his "Notes," has collected many of the Japanese proverbs. Herr Knobloch, too, in the "Transactions of the German Society of Japan," has done much in this direction, whilst Sir Edward J. Reed's important work on "Japan: its History, Traditions, and Religions" (1880, 2 vols.) has devoted a chapter to the proverbs and proverbial sayings current among the Japanese people, in many of which he says, "there is in the original a play upon words which cannot be translated, but which sharpens the point of the phrase to the native"—a remark, however, which applies to most translations of foreign proverbs. When we turn to Japanese wisdom relative to woman's beauty, we find much the same advice given as is found amongst Western nations, one of their popular admonitions reminding us that "the heart is better than a beautiful face"—in other words, it is far better for a woman to have a good heart than to have a beautiful face; and the danger that often lurks behind a pretty face has been incorporated into many of their proverbs, one of which runs thus : "Beware of beautiful women as you would of red pepper" ; and, it may be added, even the Japanese have long ago commented in their proverbial lore on woman's loquacity, one of their household maxims reaffirming what, under one form or another, seems to be universally acknowledged—that "a woman's tongue three inches long can kill a man six feet high."

Among some of the other works to which we have been more or less indebted in the succeeding pages may be mentioned the following : J. Christian's "Behar Proverbs" ; A. Manwaring's "Marathi Proverbs" ; "Telugu Proverbs," by Narasimha Acharyulu ; "Sindhi Proverbs," by Rochiram Gajumal ; "English Proverbs, with Urdu Equivalents," by Wazir Ahmad ; "Osmanli Proverbs," by Ahmad Midhat (1898) ; and W. E. Taylor's "African Aphorisms" (1891).

T. F. THISELTON-DYER.

CONTENTS

CHAPTER XV

CHAPTER XVI

CHAPTER XVII

CHAPTER XVIII

CHAPTER XIX

CHAPTER XX

CHAPTER XXI

CHAPTER XXII

CHAPTER XXIII

CHAPTER XXIV

CHAPTER XXV

CHAPTER XXVI

CHAPTER XXVII

CHAPTER I

WOMAN'S CHARACTERISTICS

It is only a woman that can make a man become the parody of himself.—*French Proverb.*

PROVERBIAL philosophy has long agreed that woman is a complex creature, little understood, and, according to Michelet, "she is a miracle of Divine contradictions;" an opinion endorsed by Pope, who in his "Moral Essays,"[1] writes, "Woman's at best a contradiction still;" and, further, by Richter,[2] who says, "A woman is the most inconsistent compound of obstinacy and self-sacrifice that I am acquainted with." The wisest sages from the earliest period have been forced to admit that he would be a truly clever man who could understand, and account for, the many and varied characteristics of womankind, for, as Lord Byron wrote:—

"What a strange thing is man! And what a stranger
Is woman! What a whirlwind is her head!
And what a whirlpool, full of depth and danger,
Is all the rest about her! Whether wed

---

[1] Ep. ii., line 270.
[2] "Flower, Fruit, and Thorn."

> Or widow, maid or mother, she can change her
> Mind like the wind ; whatever she has said
> Or done, is light to what she shall say or do—
> The oldest thing on record, and yet new." [1]

And yet it is universally acknowledged that woman is indispensable to man's happiness and well-being, for, as it is said in Germany, " Man without woman is head without body, woman without man is body without head," which corresponds with the French adage, " Without woman the two extremes of life would be without help, and the middle of it without pleasure ; " and, long ago, the Egyptians were wont to represent a man without a woman by a single millstone, which cannot grind alone. The Burmese, too, of to-day maintain that " of all beings woman is most excellent ; she is the chief of supporters ;" [2] and, according to another of their proverbial maxims, " her intelligence is four times that of man, her assiduity six times, and her desires eight times." Eastern proverbs are highly complimentary to women ; for whereas, says a Sanskrit adage, " they are instructed by nature, the learning of men is taught by books ; " or, as another piece of Oriental wisdom reminds us, " Nature is woman's teacher, and she learns more sense than man, the pedant, gleams from books." [3] And, in short, the power and influence

[1] " Don Juan," canto ix. st. 64.

[2] See the " Nîti Literature of Burma," by James Gray, 1886, p. 71.

[3] See the Rev. T. Long's " Eastern Proverbs and Emblems," 1881, p. 7.

of woman have been admirably described by Thomas Otway in his "Venice Preserved" (act i. sc. 1):—

> "O woman! lovely woman! Nature made thee
> To temper man; we had been brutes without you.
> Angels are painted fair to look like you"—

which is somewhat at variance with a popular Russian proverb to the effect that "the man is head of the woman, but she rules him by her temper;" and with the Spanish maxim, "A woman's counsel is not much, but he that despises it is a fool;" and again, with the Hindustani proverb, "Woman is wise when too late." But it would appear that, in summing up the characteristics of woman, proverbial lore, taken as a whole, is far more favourably disposed to her good points than the reverse, as is clearly the case with that of our French neighbours, who, long ago, have freely admitted the power of her influence in the world. Thus we are told that "women can do everything, because they rule those who command everything;" and "Women are the extreme, they are either better or worse than men;" and, again, it is said, "The world is the book of women"—a Kashmiri proverb truly maintaining that "One woman is wealth to you, another ruination."

Woman has often been said to be equal to any emergency, a German saying expressing this idea thus: "Though an elephant and a tiger come she will leap over them;" and Hindustani lore waxes eloquent on this point—"What cannot a woman do? What cannot the ocean contain?

What cannot the fire burn? What cannot death destroy?"

Most Oriental proverbs are much to the same effect, and it is said that "None know the wily tricks of a woman; they will kill their husbands, and then burn themselves," in order to prove their innocence; and again we are told, "Women's wills and thieves' tricks cannot be fathomed." And an old Welsh proverb warns us against the artifices of womankind, for—

> "Nothing earthly hath a way
> Like a woman to betray;"

and Hindustani lore tells us that "Womankind is perfidious;" and much to the same purport is the Assamese saying—

> "Of women, Miris, the parrot, and the crow,
> The minds of these four you cannot know;"

for the Assamese never trust women; and not very complimentary is the Hindu saying, "My lady drops a spark in the chaff, and stands off to see the fun." Another common notion, underlying the proverbial lore relating to women, is their meanness—an amusing illustration of which may be quoted from Hindustani maxims, one of which runs thus: "Three cakes of a pennyweight each, and all her friends to eat them." But the reason for this frequent trait of character has been assigned to a woman's proverbial love of money, for—

> "Nothing agreeth worse
> Than a lady's heart and a beggar's purse."

But, it must be remembered, another proverb tells us that—

> "Weal and women cannot pan
> But woe and women can"—

"pan" being equivalent to harmonise.

Proverbial philosophy is full of warning against forming hastily an estimate of women's character, for, as the German adage runs, "He must have keen eyes that would know a maid at sight." We are further told that a woman should be seen at home, when engaged in her household duties, to form a clear estimate of her character; and the Danish proverb inculcates this rule: "You must judge a maiden at the kneading trough, and not at the dance."

That two women seldom keep friends for long without quarrelling has long been proverbial, and a Tamil adage remarks that "A thousand men may live together in harmony, whereas two women are unable to do so though they be sisters." And the many ailments to which, under one form or another, women are supposed to be susceptible, have been incorporated into many a proverb like the following: "A mill, a clock, and a woman, always want mending."

It has long been said that there is no accounting for a woman's tastes, and, according to an old English proverb, "A black man is a jewel in a fair woman's eyes;" and, *vice versâ*, we are told that "A black woman hath turpentine in her," a belief which has been told in various ways, an old proverbial phrase quoted by Hazlitt giving this advice—

> "To a red man read thy read;
> With a brown man break thy bread;
> At a pale man draw thy knife,
> From a black man keep thy wife"—

in illustration of which he gives the subjoined note from Tofte's translation of Varchi's "Blazon of Jealousie" (1615, p. 21):—"The Persians were wont to be so jealous of their wives, as they never suffered them to go abroad but in waggons close shut, but at this day the Italian is counted the man that is most subject to this vice, the sallow-complexioned fellow with a black beard, being he that is most prone, as well to suspect, as to be suspected about women's matters, according to the old saying."

It would seem that, in early times, the fair sex were supposed to have the greater charms, and accordingly they were styled, "Children of the Gods" by the Greeks. In "As you Like it" (act iii. sc. 5), the Shepherdess Phœbe complains of being scorned on account of her being dark—

> "I have more cause to hate him than to love him:
> For what had he to do to chide at me?
> He said mine eyes were black and my hair black:
> And, now I am remember'd, scorned at me."[1]

Indeed, as a writer has observed in the *Saturday Review*, the time was when the black-haired,

[1] See Chapter on the "Eyes."

black-eyed girl of fiction was as dark of soul as of tresses, while the blue-eyed maiden's character was of "Heaven's own colour." But Thackeray changed this tradition by invariably making his dark heroines nice, his fair heroines "treacherous sirens." Another item of folk-lore tells us that—

> "A brown wench in face
> Shows that nature gives her grace,"

and many of our country peasantry still affirm that "a too brown lass is gay and cleanly;" whilst, in accordance with an old proverbial rhyme—

> "The red is wise, the brown trusty,
> The pale envious, the dark lusty."

Dr. Paul Topinard, in his "Anthropology," has made an interesting summary of the variation of the colour of the skin, from the fairest Englishwoman to the darkest African, furnishing us with numerous examples of the many hues which form the distinguishing marks of different nationalities. These are interesting if only as showing how widely one country differs from another in its notion as to what constitutes beauty in the complexion. And, turning to uncultured tribes, Dr. Letourneau has given some curious illustrations in his "Sociology" on this point, which show how vastly different are their conceptions of beauty of complexion, some races even disfiguring themselves with pigments of the most glaring colours.

French proverbial wisdom in further enumerating the main features of a woman's character, says that her heart is a real mirror, which "reflects every object without attaching itself to any;" and in Germany, whilst due praise is bestowed on the fair sex, women's varied traits of character have not escaped criticism—one very common maxim affirming that "she is at the mercy of circumstances just as the sand is at the mercy of the wind;" whilst we are further told that, although "woman reads and studies endlessly, her thought is always an afterthought." The Russian is of the same opinion, for, according to him, "a woman's hair is long, but her sense short," and "a dog is wiser than a woman, he does not bark at his master." Tamil proverbial wisdom declares that "the skill of a woman only goes so far as the fireplace"—in other words, cleverness is no use to a woman outside domestic affairs; and the not very complimentary old English adage says, "When an ass climbs a ladder, we may find wisdom in a woman;" whilst another old saying runs, "She hath less beauty than her picture, and truly not much more wit."

In some instances, we find the essential requirements needed to make a good woman laid down, as in an excellent Chinese proverb, which runs thus: "We ask four things for a woman—that virtue dwell in her heart, modesty in her forehead, sweetness in her mouth, and labour in her hands;" with which may be compared a well-known Sanskrit maxim, "The beauty of the cuckoo is the voice, of women chastity; of the deformed learning, and of ascetics patience." On the other hand, under a variety of forms, proverbial literature inculcates the necessity of our remembrance of these four evils thus summed up in the Italian warning : " From four things God preserve us—a painted woman, a conceited valet, salt beef without mustard, and a little late dinner." A similar idea is conveyed in the Assamese proverb : " To be the husband of a worthless woman, a cart covering with a hole in the middle of it, a hired weaver—these three are the agony of death." To understand this proverb it must be remembered that " in Assam the bullock cart is covered with a hood made of matting, with bamboo hoops to support it. Any one who has travelled in a bullock cart with a hole in the hood will appreciate its truth."

A trait of character, however, which women are proverbially said to their disadvantage to possess, is a lack of truth and reliability; and, according to an old proverb, " He who takes an eel by the tail, or a woman at her word, soon finds he holds nothing." The popular adage which warns a man not to trust a woman further than he can see her has been variously expressed, one version in Germany being " Arms, women, and books should be looked at daily;" and, according to another, it is said, " Beware of a bad woman, and put no trust in a good one;" which are similar to the Hindustani adage, " A hare and a woman are yours while in your power." The Italians have a maxim to the same effect, " Woman always speak the truth, but not the whole truth," and hence there are the frequent admonitions against trusting womankind, for the French affirm that " he who trusts a woman and leads an ass will never be free from plague;" and, similarly, it is said, "The ruses of women multiply with their years;" and where truth is deficient in a woman there can be no reliance in her word, for, as the Chinese affirm, "An untruthful woman is rotten grass and tangled hemp." But, unreliable as a woman at times may be, we cannot endorse the Turkish maxim, "The dog is faithful, woman never;" which is not unlike the Kashmiri proverb: "A horse, a wife, and a sword, these three are unfaithful;" and Hindu proverbial literature, speaking of woman's insincerity, says that "while the wife is eating her husband's food, she is inwardly singing the praises of her mother."

On the other hand, in defence of woman, it has been urged that good-nature and simplicity of character are liable to imposition, for, as it is commonly said, "All lay load on the winning horse," a version of which is to be found among Sindhi proverbs: "A mild-faced woman has her cheeks pulled." We may further compare our own proverbs: "She is as quiet as a wasp in one's nose," and "She looks as if butter would not melt in her mouth;" and, again, "A gentle housewife mars the household"—in other words, through her leniency there is "a want of discipline."

An amusing phrase to denote a proud woman is this, "She holds up her head like a hen drinking water;" and when Herefordshire folk speak of a strong, robust girl, the remark may still occasionally be heard, "She hath one point of a good hawk, she is hardy." When a girl simpers and puts on an affected appearance, in such a way as to excite ridicule and amusement, she is still, in old proverbial phraseology, said to "simper as a mare when she eats thistles," or to "simper like a furmity kettle." An indolent girl is described as "having broken her elbow," and the phrase applied to a woman who grows inactive after marriage is, "She hath broken her elbow at the church-door." The same idea, again, is conveyed in the adage, "She had rather kiss than spin," implying that many a young girl, instead of being industrious at home, would much sooner gad about and play with love; and, if this be not in her power, to use a Somersetshire phrase, "She is as crusty as that is hard-baked."

Chastity, to which references will be found in ensuing chapters, has been universally regarded as an essential necessity for a good woman, for as a popular proverb, current under a variety of forms in most countries, enjoins, "An immodest woman is food without salt;" and a Chinese maxim tells us that "modesty is a woman's courage;" whereas Tacitus wrote in his day, "When a woman has lost her character, she will shrink from no crime." And, where this trait of character is wanting, the consensus of opinion seems to be that no amount of care, or foresight, will prevent a woman going astray; for a Kural saying, too, teaches much the same lesson—

"Of what avail are prisons barred,
Their chastity is women's guard."

And a Malay proverb emphasises the tenacity of

a woman's purpose, whether that be good or bad—

> "A whole herd of buffaloes might be shut up in a pen,
> There is one thing not to be guarded—a woman."

Much to the same effect is the Eastern proverb, "Women, if confined at home by faithful guardians, are not really guarded; but those women who guard themselves by their own will, are well guarded," to which may be added the German adages: "A sackful of fleas is easier to watch than a woman," and "A woman and a glass are always in danger;" whilst the old English proverbial phrase, "She will stay at home, perhaps, if her leg be broken," implies that nothing but what happens through compulsion will keep many a woman at home. Indeed, it has always been held that there is no compensation for the lack of chastity in a woman, an old Tamil maxim declaring that "beauty without chastity is a flower without fragrance."

On the other hand, an Arabic proverb says that "The modest woman's walk lasts from morning till evening," which has been thus explained, "The modest woman rarely goes out, or meets any one, and, when she does get the opportunity to go out, she is as delighted with the various sights as if she were a stranger, and she spends a long time in looking at them, and in chatting with those of her intimate friends whom she meets, so that the length of her absence from the house has become proverbial." [1]

Lastly, due consideration for the frailty of woman is extensively enjoined in proverbial lore, a Tamil adage telling us that "though you see a woman sin with your own eyes, cover it over with earth," for, it adds, "if she says, I am a woman, even the devil will have compassion on her;" and hence a person is sternly warned "not to dare to stand on the earth when passing unjust remarks on a woman." A German proverb says, "Frailty, thy name is woman," which is to the same effect as the Eastern aphorism, "Women, like flowers, are of tender fabric, and should be softly handled;" which coincides with the Indian maxim, "Do not strike, even with a flower, a woman guilty of a hundred crimes," and with the Hindustani proverb, "It is not right to lift one's hand to a woman."

At the same time, our forefathers were strongly of opinion that a certain amount of correction was good for women, an opinion to which we have referred in our chapter on "Woman's Goodness," where we have given some of the proverbial wisdom on the subject. Among Oriental proverbs too much leniency is deprecated, it being said that "the petted boy becomes a gambler, and the petted girl a wanton," which is similar to the Marathi maxim, "By the mother's petting the child becomes an idiot;" and to our own proverbs "A child may have too much of his mother's blessing," and "Mothers' darlings make but milk-

[1] See J. R. Jewett's "Arabic Proverbs," American Oriental Society, 1891, vol. xv.

sop heroes;" for, says Ray, "Mothers are oftentimes too tender and fond of their children, who are ruined and spoiled by their indulgence." In Hindustani lore we find the same idea expressed, a familiar adage maintaining that, "Melons require the sun, and mangoes want the sun; women need a strong hand, and children want love." The reason for this would seem to be that a woman does not always know what is best for her, hence the Welsh adage:—

"A woman mostly will prefer
The thing that is the worst for her."

And hence, as the Italians say, "Women, apes, and nuts require strong hands." There is an African proverb which says that "a man is not obeyed by his wife in his own house," which, we are told, implies that she does not consider him her husband "unless he beat her, thwack"—a mode of treatment which, it is needless to say, would not be endured by the wives of the West.[1]

[1] See W. E. Taylor's "African Aphorisms," 1891.

CHAPTER II

WOMAN'S BEAUTY

"She's beautiful and therefore to be wooed;
She is a woman, therefore to be won."
1st Henry VI. act v. sc. 3.

"A BEAUTIFUL woman," remarked Napoleon, "pleases the eye, a good woman pleases the heart; one is a jewel, the other a treasure." It is not surprising that the beauty of woman—in praise of which both literature and art have from the earliest period lavished some of their grandest works—should have given rise in most countries to a host of strange and romantic fancies. Many of these survive in our midst to-day, and, although experience has long proved how unreliable such beliefs are, they still retain their hold on the popular mind, often causing unnecessary prejudice and fear.

It is a very old notion, for instance, that beauty is unfortunate; and, according to an old Italian proverb, "Over the greatest beauty hangs the greatest ruin." Allusions to this piece of folk-lore are not only found in the poetry and romance of bygone centuries, but are of frequent occurrence in the literature of modern times. Thus Goëthe makes Helena affirm that "beauty and happiness remain not long united;" and Byron, in his "Childe Harold" (iv. 42), speaks of "the fatal gift of beauty." We may recall, too, Lord Tennyson's charming and pathetic language in "A Dream of Fair Women," where he relates how—

> "In every land
> I saw, wherever light illumineth,
> Beauty and anguish walking hand in hand
> The downward slope to death.
>
> Those far-renowned brides of ancient song
> Peopled the hollow dark, like burning stars,
> And I heard sounds of insult, shame, and wrong,
> And trumpets blown for wars."

And there is a well-known passage where Fielding, in his "Journey from this World to the Next," (chap. vi.), thus writes: "She—Fortune—was one of the most deformed females I ever beheld, nor could I help observing the frowns she expressed when any beautiful spirit of her own sex passed her, nor the affability that smiled on her countenance on the approach of any handsome male spirits. Hence I accounted for the truth of an observation I had often made on earth, that nothing is more fortunate than handsome men, nor more unfortunate than handsome women;" such, too, was the opinion of the host of the "Canterbury Tales" who bewailed the sad fate of Virginia related by the Doctor of Physic :—

> "Allas ! too deare boughte sshe her beauté,
> Wherefore I say, that alle men may se,
> That giftes of fortune, or of nature,
> Ben cause of deth of many a creature.
> Her beauté was hir deth, I dar well sayn,
> Allas ! so piteously as she was slayn." [1]

And there is the old mythical tale which tells how Medusa was a maiden of such beauty as to provoke the jealousy of Minerva, wherefore she was transformed into a frightful monster. Her much-admired ringlets became hissing serpents, and no living thing could look upon her without being turned into stone. Legendary lore provides us with many stories of this kind, which illustrates Patterson's well-known lines :—

> "O fatal beauty ! why art thou bestowed
> On hapless woman still to make her wretched ?
> Betrayed by thee, how many are undone !"

Chinese folk-lore maintains that beautiful women are unlucky, one of their many proverbs on the subject declaring that "fair maidens are very unlucky, and clever young men have little beauty." It was also supposed that feminine beauty of unusual merit was fatal to long life, and no subject has been more popular with the novelist, or poet, than the gradual fading away of some young girl gifted in a high degree with good looks.

[1] L. 1378.—Ed. Wright.

Lord Tennyson, in his "May Queen," has interwoven this idea, and it is found scattered here and there in the literature of most countries. Hence, another reason why beauty has been regarded as unfortunate is owing to its being thought prejudicial to health, a variation of which belief occurs in "Richard III." (act iii. sc. 1), where the Duke of Gloucester says:—

> "So wise, so young, they say do never live long."

Another misfortune connected with beauty is its evanescence, and, as the German proverbs run, "Woman's beauty, the forest echo and rainbows, soon pass away," and "Maidens and roses soon lose their bloom." And the same truth is conveyed in the Hindustani proverb, "The spring in which he saw the blossoms is gone, now, O bee, only the thorns remain on the rose;" another version of which is, "My fair one don't be proud of your complexion, it is the guest of but a few days." Poets have largely dwelt on beauty's transient character, and Shakespeare, in "The Passionate Pilgrim," says:—

> "Beauty is but a vain and doubtful good;
> A shining gloss that vadeth suddenly;
> A flower that dies when first it 'gins to bud,
> A brittle glass that's broken presently,
> A doubtful good, a gloss, a glass, a flower,
> Lost, vaded, broken, dead within an hour."

And the oft-quoted adage that "Beauty is like an almanac; if it last a year it is well," reminds us of Moliere's lines in his "Les Femmes Savantes" :—

> "La beauté du visage est un frêle ornement,
> Une fleur passagére, un éclat d'un moment,
> Et qui n'est attachè qu' à la simple epiderne."

The snares of beauty have been made from early times the subject of much preverbial wisdom, a Servian adage affirming that, "Better sometimes a woman blind than one too beautiful;" for, as the Italian proverb adds, "Tell a woman that she is beautiful, and the devil will repeat it to her ten times;" with which may be compared an old Welsh proverb, which has been translated thus :—

> "Three things may make a woman nought,
> A giddy brain,
> A heart that's vain,
> A face in beauty's fashion wrought;"

and the German proverb adds, "An impudent face never marries." There is, too, the old English adage, "The fairest silk is soon stained;" for, as Ray has said, "The handsomest women are soonest corrupted, because they are most tempted."

Although we cannot endorse the old German proverb which says that, "Every woman would be rather pretty than pious," yet most women are mightily proud of their beauty, for, as an early English maxim reminds us, "She that is born a beauty is born married;" another version of which we find in an old work entitled, "New Help to Discourse" (1721, p. 134), "Beauty draws more than five yoke of oxen;" with which we may compare Pope's lines in "The Rape of the Lock" (Canto ii.):—

> "Fair tresses man's imperial race insnare,
> And beauty draws us with a single hair."

The same idea occurs in French proverbial lore, but it is thus qualified :—

> "Amour fait beaucoup
> Mais argent fait tout ;"

and according to German proverbial lore, "Beauty is a good letter of introduction," and, "Good looks are an inheritance," and again, "A pretty face is a good drummer;" but, on the other hand, it is said, "A poor beauty finds more lovers than husbands."

It is not surprising that in all ages women have striven to preserve their beauty, however transient it may be, for, as it has been remarked, "it is valueless to a woman to be young unless pretty, or to be pretty unless young;" and an amusing story is told of an old queen who, day after day, sighed with longing regret that her beauty had vanished, and that her young days were gone. In this sad dilemma she was advised to try some magic restorative to bring back the rosy blush of youth, and accordingly—

> "Of rosmayr she took six pounde,
> And grounde it well into a stownde,"

and then she mixed with it water, in which she bathed three times a day, taking care to anoint her head with "gode balme afterwards." In a few days her old withered face fell away, and she became so young and pretty that she began to look out for a husband.

But, unfortunately, stories of this class belong to the domain of fairyland, or, otherwise, old age would have a bad time of it, for every woman would remain young if not beautiful. At any rate, there is no disguising the fact that the human brain has done its very best to accommodate the fair sex with the charm of juvenescence, judging from the rules laid down for this purpose; a popular folk-rhyme advising us thus :—

> "Those who wish to be fair and stout,
> Must wash their faces with the disclout;
> Those who wish to be wrinkled and grey,
> Must keep the disclout far away."

The common wayside flower, the lady's mantle, was once in great repute with ladies; for, according to Hoffman, it had the power of "restoring feminine beauty, however faded, to its early freshness;" and the wild tansy, laid to soak in buttermilk for nine days, had the reputation of "making the complexion very fair." The hawthorn, again, was in high repute among the fair sex, for according to an old piece of proverbial lore :—

> "The fair maid who, the first of May,
> Goes to the fields at break of day,
> And washes in dew from the hawthorn-tree,
> Will ever after handsome be";

and the common fumitory "was used when gathered in wedding hours and boiled in water, milk, and whey, as a wash for the complexion of rustic maids."[1]

Various allusions to these old recipes occur in the literature of the past, and we find the Earl of Shrewsbury—who had charge of the unfortunate Mary Queen of Scots—making an application for an increased allowance on account of her expensive habit of bathing in wine. Those who could not afford such an extravagant luxury contented themselves with milk-baths, which were all the fashion in the reign of Charles II.

Great importance, too, has long been attached to what is popularly nicknamed "Beauty Sleep," it being supposed that the two hours' sleep before midnight are worth all that comes after it, and are far more instrumental in keeping off wrinkles than all the cosmetics and expedients to which we have just referred, the faintest indication of which is a killing blow to womankind. Hence it is not surprising that, in the words of a Portuguese proverb, the marriageable young lady cries in despair, "marry me, mother, for my face is growing wrinkled." The explanation given by Ray of the value of the so-called beauty-sleep is amusing: "For the sun being the light of this sublunary world, whose heat causes the motion of all terrestrial animals, when he is farthest off, that is about midnight, the spirits of themselves are aptest to rest and compose, so that the middle of the night must needs be the most proper time to sleep in, especially if we consider the greater expense of spirits in the daytime, partly by the heat of the afternoon, and partly by

1 Black's "Folk Medicine," p. 201.

labour, and the constant exercise of all the senses; whereof then to wake is put the spirits in motion, when there are fewest of them, and they naturally most sluggish and unfit for it."

But it is generally acknowledged that the attempt to cheat time of his wrinkles has nearly always proved fruitless, and only too frequently "the would-be fair ones have been driven in despair to conceal what they found it impossible to remove, and hence the feminine fashion of bedaubing the complexion with artificial tints, a custom which it may be remembered was almost universal among Grecian women."

On the other hand, however much fortune may be reputed to be hostile to beauty, good looks have been termed "a woman's glory," and Galen perhaps was not far wrong in maintaining that one reason why misfortune is so often connected with beauty is that "many who have been distinguished for their loveliness have neglected the education of their mind," for, as the German proverbs say, "Beauty and understanding go rarely together;" "Beauty is but dross if honesty be lost," and there is the Tamil adage, "Beauty in the unworthy is poison in a casket of gold." Some, like Ralph Nickleby, may disparage a woman's beauty, but, as it has been remarked, one reason why beauty has been coveted by most women is partly owing to the early belief that a lovely face was the outward indication that a person so adorned was gifted with an equally beautiful soul within. It was long and extensively believed that a lofty soul could not dwell in an ugly casket, and hence a beautiful woman was commonly credited with having a fine and noble character, a notion which in only too many instances history alone has refuted, for, as an old proverb says, "Beauty may have fair leaves, but little fruit." This once popular belief, however, was a favourite one with the poets, and is referred to in the "Tempest," (act i. sc. 2) :—

> "There's nothing ill can dwell in such a temple :
> If the ill Spirit have so fair a house,
> Good things will strive to dwell with't."

And Young alludes to the same idea in these well-known lines :—

> "What's female beauty, but an air divine,
> Through which the mind's all gentle graces shine ?
> They, like the sun, irradiate all between,
> The body charms, because the soul is seen,
> Hence men are often captives of a face
> They know not why, of no peculiar grace.
> Some forms, though bright, no mortal man can bear,
> Some, none resist, though not exceeding fair."

Moralists and others have largely dwelt on this familiar idea, and, in one form or another, it has prevailed in most countries, and has been incorporated in many a legendary romance ; an item of folk-lore which Sir A. de Vere Hunt has thus prettily expressed :—

> "What is beauty ? not the show
> Of shapely limbs and features—no !
> These are but flowers
> That have their dated hours
> To breathe their momentary sweets, then go.
> 'Tis the stainless soul within,
> That outshines the fairest skin."

There would appear, however, to be an exception to this rule, for German folk-wisdom tells us that "A fair skin often covers a crooked mind," and "A fair face may hide a foul heart," which reminds us of the whited sepulchres of the New Testament; and it is further said in Germany that "Falseness often lurks beneath fair hair," and there is the Spanish proverb, "A handsome woman is either silly or vain."

But notions of beauty fortunately differ, and, according to a popular adage, "What is one man's meat is another man's poison;" and, whatever truth there may be in the proverb which reminds us that "Beauty is but skin deep," there is no denying that personal appearance has made all the difference in the estimation formed by one person of another. According to an old folk-rhyme we are told that:—

> "A fair face is half a portion,
> A fair face may be a foul bargain,
> A fair face may hide a foul heart,
> A fair field and no favour."

The power of woman's beauty over man, however, has always been proverbial all over the world, and, from the earliest period, it has formed one of the leading subjects of the wise-saws current in most countries. Thus a popular German maxim tells us that "one hair of a woman draws more than a bell-rope," or, as another version has it, "Beauty draws us with a single hair;" and there is a common saying in the East, "A good-looking woman in a house is the foe of all the plain ones." At the same time there have never been wanting moralists to warn us that, however powerful the fascinatory influence of woman's beauty may be, it is far from being always supreme. Accordingly there are a number of proverbs which affirm that, whereas "beauty is potent, money is omnipotent," with which may be compared the oft-quoted saying to the effect that, "Beauties without fortunes have sweethearts plenty; but husbands none at all;" or, as it is sometimes said, "Beauty without bounty avails nought." Oftentimes those proverbs, which admit the fascinatory charms of a woman's beauty, qualify their statements with a warning, as in the German proverb, "Beauty is the eye's food, and the soul's sorrow;" an old English maxim is to the same effect: "A beautiful woman is the paradox of the eyes, the hell of the soul, and the purgatory of the purse;" and again, "Wickedness with beauty is the devil's hook baited;" the same idea being found in Hindustani proverbial wisdom, in which we find this maxim: "All pretty maids are poisonous pests; an enemy kills by hiding these by smiles and jests." It is said in Italy that "a beautiful woman smiling bespeaks a purse-weeping," with which may be compared the German adage:—

> "Hares are caught with hounds,
> Fools with praises,
> Women with gold."

Indeed, in most countries there are numerous proverbs to the same effect, demonstrating how one of the penalties—one which oftentimes is man's ruin—paid for woman's beauty is an empty purse. Similarly, we are told that "a handsome hostess is bad for the purse;" and hence there is some truth in the following: "A rich man is never ugly in the eyes of a girl."

Proverb-making cynics, again, have not always been very chivalrous and complimentary in their allusions to the charms of the fair sex. Thus, as beautiful women had the reputation of being less handy and serviceable than plain ones, the adage arose which says—"A fair woman and a slashed gown will always find some nail in the way;" in other words, as women value themselves on their personal attractions, they are in the same degree generally apt to be negligent in other things. According to another version of the same proverb, it is very commonly said that "the more women look in their glasses the less they look to their houses." Cynical sayings, happily, of this kind, as far as beauty is concerned, are in the minority; for, in most legendary and historical lore, good features have been made characteristic of nearly all superior and exalted beings. Hence, at the present day, beauty is often said to be "fairylike," it having been a popular belief that beauty, united with power, was one of the most attractive forms of the fairy tribe. Such was that of Spenser's Fairy Queen, and of Shakespeare's Titania; and it may be remembered how, in "Antony and Cleopatra" (act iv. sc. 8), Antony, on seeing Cleopatra enter, says to Scarus:—

> "To this great fairy I'll commend thy acts,
> Make her thanks bless thee."

And in "Cymbeline" (act iii. sc. 6), when the two brothers find Imogen in their cave, Belarius exclaims :—

> "But that it eats our victuals, I should think
> Here were a fairy,"

and he then adds :—

> "By Jupiter, an angel! or, if not,
> An earthly paragon! Behold divineness,
> No elder than a boy."

Beauty, too, which Plato described as "a privilege of Nature;" Homer, "a glorious gift of Nature;" Ovid, "a favour bestowed by the Gods;" and Shakespeare, "that miracle and queen of gems," has formed the theme of most of those traditionary tales of love and romance which, embodied in the folk-tales of different countries, portray the many beliefs and fancies which, in the course of centuries, have grouped round this acknowledged charm of womanhood.

The absence of beauty, on the other hand, was, in days of old, considered almost a disgrace, it having been a common idea that the ugliness of the wicked was in proportion to their evil nature. Hence, an unprepossessing appearance subjected the unfortunate woman to the most uncomplimentary stigma, and oftentimes even made her an object of contempt; for, according to an old proverb, "An ugly woman is a disease of the stomach, a handsome woman a disease of the head." And there is the Hebrew adage, "Ugliness is the guardian of women," for the chance is remote of those who are not gifted with beauty yielding to the snares of temptation. But even ugliness occasionally outweighs the advantages of beauty, for the German mother reminds her daughter that "a virtuous woman, though ugly, is the ornament of her house;" and there is the Spanish adage, which says, "the ugliest is the best housewife;" and our own proverb runs: "She's better than she's bonnie;" although a Tamil proverb, referring ironically to an ugly woman, speaks of her as "killed with beauty;" and a Welsh adage tells us that if an ugly woman fall, breaking her hip, the pity she gets is, "how clumsy to trip." It has, however, been generally acknowledged that there is no woman who is not, more or less, fond of flattery, and there is a common saying in Spain, "Tell a woman she is pretty and you will turn her head," a piece of proverbial lore which is found in France and Germany, and also in our own country. But, after all, there is one point to be remembered, for a popular German adage says that "handsome women generally fall to the lot of ugly men." There is truth, also, in the Sindhi adage, which says, "Better a blind eye than a blind fate," which means, better be ugly than unfortunate, as many favoured with beauty are supposed to be; for, after all, as the proverb truly remarks, "a good fame is better than a good face." It is recorded that Madame de Bourignon was so ugly when born that the proposal was actually made of smothering her, so as to spare her a life of ridicule and humiliation; and, to quote a further illustration, a story is told of the Emperor Henry IV., of Germany, who, on entering a church, where an ugly priest happened to be officiating, wondered in his mind whether it was possible for God to accept services rendered by so ill-favoured a ministrant. But the imperial ministrations were interrupted by the priest's boy mumbling, almost unintelligibly, the versicle : "It is He that hath made us, not we ourselves," whereupon the priest removed him for his indistinct enunciation, and he repeated the Psalmist's words, which the Emperor took as an undesigned rebuke to his own thoughts.

Queen Elizabeth, similarly, was careful to admit into her household none but those of "stature and birth ;" and one day, it is recorded, she went so far as to refuse the services of a certain individual for no other reason than that one of his jaws was deficient of a tooth ! But there was Tamerlane's wife, who, although she had no nose, was considered a belle by her contemporaries ; and even hunchbacks have had their admirers on the ground that the "dorsal curvature is the true line of beauty."

It has, after all, however, been generally admitted that beauty is, more or less, deceptive, and especially where love is concerned, for, as the popular adage says : "If Jack is in love, he is no judge of Jill's beauty," which corresponds with the Italian saying, "Handsome is not what is handsome, but what pleases." Similarly, the French have a familiar proverb, "Never seemed a prison fair, nor a mistress foul," which has its counterpart in Germany, where it is said, "he whose fair one squints says she ogles;" and "Everybody thinks his own cuckoo sings better than another's nightingale;" with which we may compare what the African negro says, "The beetle is a beauty in the eyes of its mother"—love transforming all imperfections into beauty. But, as an Eastern piece of proverbial wisdom reminds us—

> "For virtue a woman our wife we make;
> For her beauty we a concubine take,"

with which may be compared another Eastern adage:—

> "Long not for the Goddess's beauty divine,
> Long that the star of your husband may shine."

The fact that love has a large mantle to hide faults is further shown in an Arab proverb: "Love is the companion of blindness;" and the Talmud emphasises the same truth: "To love a thing makes the eye blind, the ear deaf;" and a Hindustani proverb runs thus: "Fall in love with an ogress, and even she is a fairy," with which may be compared another not very complimentary one, "Her name is Beauty, and a dog's her face." It is interesting to find the same idea in Assamese folk-lore, wherein occurs the following: "What shall I say of my step-mother's character—in one hand she has chutney and in the other salt; she has no hair in the middle of her head, but her husband calls her the beautiful one?" And much the same idea is conveyed in the Hindustani piece of proverbial wisdom: "She cries over her own idiot, but laugh's at another's ;" and the Dutch have a saying, "No ape but swears he has the handsomest children."

Indeed, that in a lover's eyes, plainness oftentimes becomes actual beauty, is exemplified over and over again in the literature of past and modern days, for, in "A Midsummer Night's Dream" (act v. sc. 1)—

"The lover, all as frantic,
Sees Helen's beauty in a brow of Egypt."

Lord Lytton, in "Kenelm Chillingly," has introduced the charming song, "The Beauty of the Mistress is in the Lover's Eye," which runs thus:—

"Is she not pretty, my Mabel May?
Nobody ever yet called her so.
Are not her lineaments faultless, say?
If I must answer you plainly—No.

Joy to believe that the maid I love
None but myself as she is can see;
Joy that she steals from her heaven above,
And is only revealed on this earth to me."

The same idea is introduced in Mrs. Browning's "My Kate;" and Balzac, too, was of the same opinion, for he says, "When women love, they forgive us everything, even our crimes; when they do not love us, they give us credit for nothing, not even for our virtues." But, on the other hand, there is equal truth in the Welsh proverb, which is only too frequently proved in the romance of daily life, "Faults are thick when love is thin." [1]

[1] See *Notes and Queries*, 8th S. ii. 477.

Some, again, have tried to disparage beauty by maintaining that it is only "skin-deep," a notion which has found its way into proverbial lore. The literature of the past contains sundry allusions to this idea, and in the Rev. Rob. Fleming's poems (1691) we are reminded that—

> "Beauty is but skin-thick, and so doth fall
> Short of those statues made of wood or stone."

And in Ralph Venning's "Orthodoxe Paradoxe" (1650) it is said that—

> "All the beauty of the world 'tis but skin-deep, a sunne-blast defaceth;"

which is not unlike Sir Thomas Overbury's lines in his poem, "A Wife"—

> "And all the carnall beauty of my wife
> Is but skin-deep."[1]

And yet there is much truth in the Hindu adage, "The eyes love beauty, the heart loves wisdom," for, as it has been observed elsewhere, there is no denying the truth of the old French proverb, "It is not the greatest beauties that inspire the most profound passion;" and to the same purport is the German adage, "One cannot live on beauty."

[1] See *Notes and Queries*, 6th, xii. 127.

CHAPTER III

WOMAN'S DRESS

"A lovely woman, garmented in light."
SHELLEY, *The Witch of Atlas*.

"THE true ornament of a woman," writes Justin, "is virtue, not dress;" but the love of finery, whether rightly or wrongly, has always been held to be one of the inherent weaknesses of womankind, and an old proverb says that "'tis as natural for women to pride themselves on fine clothes as 'tis for a peacock to spread his tail," with which may be compared an Eastern proverb, "A woman without ornament is like a field without water." But, perhaps, there is some excuse for this love of vanity, especially as dress pleases the opposite sex, it being popularly supposed in Spain that "A well-dressed woman draws her husband from another woman's door." It is said in Japan that "An ugly woman dreads the mirror," and some allowance must, therefore, be made for her desire to make up, in some measure, by dress what she lacks in good looks, although the proverb runs in Italy that "ugly women finely dressed are the uglier for it." This, however, must not be regarded as the popular verdict, a Tamil aphorism being not far wrong when it recommends us to "put jewellery on a woman and to look at her, and to plaster a wall and to look at it," implying that both will be improved by care. This advice, says Mr. Jensen,[1] is generally given by a mother to one who confesses that her daughter is not exactly a beauty. Even Ovid was forced to complain that "dress is most deceptive, for, covered with jewels and gold ornaments everywhere, a girl is often the least part of herself;" with which may be compared the expression of Euripides, which is to this effect, "She who dresses for others beside her husband, makes herself a wanton."

It has long, however, been a familiar adage in most countries that "fine feathers make fine birds"; for, as the Spanish say, "No woman is ugly when she is dressed;" and, according to the Chinese proverb, "Three-tenths of a woman's good looks are due to nature, seven-tenths to dress;" a piece of proverbial lore which holds good in most countries.

It is not surprising that woman's dress has been much caricatured by wits and satirists, and been made the subject of many a piece of proverbial lore. As Plautus observed of a certain young lady, "it's no good her being well dressed if she's badly mannered; ill-breeding mars a fine dress

[1] "Tamil Proverbs," 1897, p. 382.

more than dirt"—in other words, he meant to imply that dress is oftentimes deceptive and creates a false appearance, which is not in keeping with the woman who wears it. Many of our old proverbs are to the same effect, an oft-quoted one affirming that "fine clothes oftentimes hide a base descent," with which may be compared the following: "Fine dressing is a foul house swept before the doors," an illustration of which Ray thus gives—"Fair clothes, ornaments and dresses, set off persons and make them appear handsome, which, if stripped of them, would seem but plainly and homely. God makes and apparel shapes." Extravagant dress has been universally condemned as emblematic of bad taste, and, among Hindustani proverbs on the subject, a woman too showily dressed is described as "yellow with gold and white with pearls." A Tamil proverb, speaking of an elaborately-dressed woman, says, "It is true she is adorned with flowers and gold, but she is beaten with slippers wherever she goes;" in other words, such a woman, however well dressed, is a bad character, and must be treated with scorn; a variation of this maxim being thus: "If you dress in rags and go out, you will be an object for admiration, but, if you dress up nicely and go out, people will speak ill of you," thinking that you are an overdressed woman, and, therefore, inclined to be fast. Among German proverbs we are reminded that "A woman strong in flounces is weak in the head."

In Hindustani proverbial lore an old woman

extravagantly dressed is contemptuously described "as an old mare with a red bridle," and "a gay old woman with a mat petticoat," and, according to another proverb, when a young girl not gifted with good looks is seen elaborately dressed, it is said, "On the strength of what beauty do you deck yourself thus?"

The inconsistency of dress when the home is poor and shabby has been much censured, an Eastern proverb running thus—"Nothing in the house and she sports a topaz ring," with which may be compared another saying, "Nothing to eat or drink in the house, and the lady of it very proud."

But the chief charm of a woman's dress is consistency, as it is thus expressed in a Sindhi proverb:—

> "As the wall so the painting,
> As the face so the adornment."

Similarly, it is commonly said that "fine words dress ill deeds, and hence we are told on the Continent, "the swarthy dame, dressed fine, deceives the fair one." It may be remembered, also, that the same idea occurs in "The Taming of the Shrew" (act iv. sc. 3):—

> "What, is the jay more precious than the lark,
> Because his feathers are more beautiful?
> Or is the adder better than the eel,
> Because his painted skin contents the eye?"

Accordingly proverbial lore in most parts of the

world warns men against selecting a wife by her outward appearance, which is often deceptive ; and a common Spanish adage says, "If you want a wife choose her on Saturday, not on Sunday ; " in other words, choose her when she is not decked out in her finery, otherwise a man may regret his mistake in the words of one of Heywood's proverbs :—

> "I took her for a rose, but she breedeth a burr,
> She cometh to stick to me now in hir lacke."

On the other hand, true beauty needs no adornment, or outward display, to enhance its charms, for, as it is said in Scotland, "A bonny bride is sune buskit," that is, soon dressed, or, as the Portuguese say, "a well-formed figure needs no cloak," an adage which coincides with Thomson's poetic words :—

> "Her polished limbs
> Veiled in a simple robe, their best attire,
> Beyond the pomp of dress ; for loveliness
> Needs not the foreign aid of ornament,
> But is, when unadorn'd, adorn'd the most."

However well dressed a woman may be, her nature remains the same, for, as the French say :—

> "An ape's an ape, a varlet's a varlet,
> Though she be drest in silks and scarlet."

And, among the many German proverbs to the same effect, it is said, "The maid is such as she was bred, and tow as it was spun," and "Once a housemaid never a lady," which remind us of the popular adage, "There's no making a silk purse out of a sow's ear," and there is a Sindhi maxim which has the same moral, "Beads about the neck and the devil in heart."

Another proverb, which, under a variety of forms, is found in our own and other countries, runs thus—"Let no woman's painting breed thy heart's fainting," because women who thus adorn themselves have always been subject to reproach; for, as the old adage says, "A good face needs no paint," or, as another version has it, "Fair faces need no paint."

Such a practice as that of rouging, too, has been generally discountenanced, since it has, from a very early period, been the recognised emblem of a fast woman, for it has long been said that "A harlot's face is a painted sepulchre," and as the Italian adage runs—"Women rouge that they may not blush." Hence we are told that "A woman who paints puts up a bill to let," with which we may compare the popular adage—"A woman and a cherry are painted for their own harm." The same idea exists in most countries, and there is a Chinese proverb to this effect—"I guess that a good-looking woman needs no rouge to make her pretty;" and it is further said that, "although the rouged beauty repudiates age, she cannot come up to the bloom of youth."

As "blemishes are unseen by night," according to an old Latin proverb, when dress, artfully arranged, presents most women in their most attractive form, their admirers were warned against falling into their meshes at such a time; for, as it is still commonly said by our French neighbours, "By candlelight a goat looks a lady," and on this account we are recommended by the Italians not to choose "A jewel, or a woman, or linen, by candlelight." It may be added that this idea has given rise to a host of proverbs much to the same effect, such as, "When candles be out all cats be grey," and "Joan is as good as my lady in the dark."

It has long been proverbial that the "smith's mare and the cobbler's wife are always the worst shod," a truism which, under one form or another, is found in most countries, a Sindhi adage running thus—"Her lover, an oilman, and yet her hair dirty;" and there is the Hindu proverb, "A shoemaker's wife with bursted shoes," with which we may compare the German proverb, "Anxious about her dress, but disregarding her appearance," in connection with which we may quote Heywood's couplet:—

> "But who is worse shod than the shoemaker's wife,
> With shops full of new shoes all her life?"

and the old English proverb, "The tailor's wife is worst clad."

Woman's dress, again, has from time immemorial been strongly censured in our proverbial lore as productive of extravagance, and Ovid's words have long ago passed into a popular adage, "What madness it is to carry all one's income on one's back." Among modern poets Cowper, too, wrote in the same strain :—

> "We sacrifice to dress, till household joys
> And comforts cease. Dress drains our cellars dry,
> And keeps our larder clean ; puts out our fires,
> And introduces hunger, frost, and woe,
> Where peace and hospitality might reign."

And Chinese proverbial lore says, "Do not marry wives or concubines who are gorgeously fine." There are other disadvantages, for, whereas it is said, "Silks and satins put out the fire in the kitchen," household duties are neglected, for one of Heywood's proverbs reminds us that "the more women look into the glass the less they look to the house," a German version running thus—"a woman who looks much in the glass spins but little ;" and we may compare the French saying, "A handsome landlady is bad for the purse ;" but, on the other hand, we are told "that's the best gown that goes up and down the house." Whatever the opinion of the fair sex may be on this point, we would quote the wisdom of Shakespeare's "Taming of the Shrew," (act iv. sc. 3) :—

> "Our purses shall be proud, our garments poor,
> For 'tis the mind that makes the body rich ;
> And as the sun breaks through the darkest clouds
> So honour peereth in the meanest habit."

But, whatever censures may be passed on a woman's love of dress, she generally has some answer in defence. A puritan preacher once rebuked a young girl who had just been making her hair into ringlets, "Ah," said he, "had God intended your locks to be curled, He would have curled them for you." "When I was an infant," replied the damsel, "He did, but now I am grown up He thinks I am able to do it myself."

At the same time, slovenly dress has been equally condemned, and, according to a popular adage, "A pretty girl and a tattered garment are sure to find some hook in the way," which is similar to the Italian expression, "A handsome woman and a slashed gown;" which coincide with the old English maxim—

> "A maid oft seen, a gown oft worn,
> Are disesteemed and held in scorn."

A piece of Suffolk folk-lore tells us that "If you have your clothes mended on your back, you will be ill-spoken of," or, as they add in Sussex, "you will come to want;" and in the Isle of Man one may often hear the couplet :—

> "Snotty boy, clean man,
> Snotty girl, slut of a woman"—

the idea apparently being that a dirty, untidy girl will never improve, as she is wanting in proper pride in her appearance ; but that a dirty boy will probably improve, as a lad who is too much concerned with his looks is not likely to do much good in after life![1] It was formerly, too, a common belief in most parts of the country that clothes were, more or less, indicative of a woman's prosperity, a notion which is found in the Hindustani lore, "when the clothes are torn poverty has arrived."

[1] A. W. Moore, "Folk-lore of the Isle of Man," 1891.

There is a very prevalent belief among women that if they would secure luck with any article of dress, they must wear it for the first time at church. Equal attention is also paid by many of the fair sex to the way they put on each article of dress, as, in case of its being accidentally inside out, it is considered an omen of success. In our northern counties, again, if a young woman accidentally puts a wrong hook, or button, into the hole when dressing in the morning, it is considered to be a warning that a misfortune of some kind will befall her in the course of the day, and any mishap, however trivial, is regarded as a proof of her fears having been well founded.

Most of these childish fancies retain their hold on the fair sex, and where is the young lady to be found who is not mindful of the admonition—

> "At Easter let your clothes be new,
> Or else be sure you will it rue."

A similar belief also prevails in connection with Whitsuntide, and many a girl would consider she had forfeited her claim to good luck for the ensuing twelve months if she did not appear in "new things on Whit Sunday."

Many, also, are the strange fancies relative to colour in dress, and the time-honoured rhyme is as much in force to-day as in years long ago which tell us that—

> "Green is forsaken,
> And yellow is forsworn,
> But blue is the prettiest colour that's worn"—

a piece of folk-lore which specially appertains to weddings.

According to a folk-rhyme current in the southern counties :—

> "Those dressed in blue
> Have lovers true,
> In green and white,
> Forsaken quite."

And another old proverbial rhyme says :—

> "Blue is true, Yellow's jealous,
> Green's forsaken, Red's brazen,
> White is love, and Black is death."

From its popularity blue has held a prominent place in love philactery, and one of many rhymes says :—

> "If you love me, love me true,
> Send me a ribbon, and let it be blue ;
> If you hate me, let it be seen,
> Send me a ribbon, a ribbon of green."

Mr. Morris, in his "Yorkshire Folk-Talk" (1892, pp. 227–28), writes that in some of the North Riding dales the antipathy to green as a colour for any part of the bridal costume is still very strong. "I was once at a farmhouse in a remote district near Whitby," he says, "and when discussing olden times and customs with an elderly dame was informed there were many she knew in her younger days who would rather have gone to the church to be married in their common everyday costume than in a green dress. My informant, however, was evidently one of those who held the same faith on this point as her lady companions, for she instanced a case that had come under her own observation where the bride was rash enough to be married in green, but it was added that she afterwards contracted a severe illness."

Blue, again, would appear to be in ill-favour for the wedding dress, as the bride—

> "If dressed in blue,
> She's sure to rue."

And yet in Leicestershire it is said that a bride on her wedding day should wear—

> "Something new,
> Something blue,
> Something borrowed ;"

or, as a Lancashire version puts it—

> "Something old and something new,
> Something borrowed and something blue."

The various articles of a woman's clothing, too, have their separate fancies attached to them, which, in some instances, have not only been incorporated by our peasantry in local jingles and rhymes, but occasionally have been made the subject of childish similes. Thus the poppy is commonly said to have a red petticoat and a green gown, the daffodil a yellow petticoat and green gown, and so on, fanciful ideas of this kind being expressed in many of our nursery couplets, as in the following—

> "Daffadown-dilly is come up to town,
> In a yellow petticoat and a green gown"; [1]

with which may be compared a Hindustani doggerel, the accuracy of which is only too true:—

> "Says the hemp, I am of gorgeous hue;
> Says the poppy, I am king of the world;
> But says the opium, I am a lady-love,
> Who takes me once takes me for ever." [2]

A well-known saying in Leicestershire of another class says "Shake a Leicestershire woman by the petticoat, and the beans will rattle in her throat," an expression which originated in the large quantity of that grain grown in this county, which caused it to be nicknamed "Bean Belly Leicestershire." There is another version applied to the opposite sex, which runs thus "Shake a Leicestershire man by the collar, and you shall hear the beans rattle in his belly." [3]

If a young woman's petticoats are longer than her dress this is an indication that her mother does not love her so much as her father; and, according to a Yorkshire belief, when a married woman's apron falls off it is a sign that something is coming to vex her; but should the apron of an

[1] "Domestic Folk-lore," pp. 84–85.
[2] See S. W. Fallon, "Hindustani Proverbs."
[3] See Southey's "Common Place Book," 1851, 4th Series, 341.

unmarried girl drop down she is frequently the object of laughter, as there is no surer sign that she is thinking about her sweetheart. In Suffolk the big blue apron usually worn by cottage women is known by them as a "mantle," and it is considered an omen of ill-luck if their mantle strings come untied.[1]

Odd beliefs of this kind might easily be enumerated, for even a pin is an object of superstition with most women, who invariably, on seeing one, pick it up for the sake of good luck, as, by omitting to do so, they run into imminent danger of incurring misfortune, a notion embodied in the subjoined familiar rhyme :—

> "See a pin and pick it up,
> All the day you'll have good luck ;
> See a pin and let it lie,
> All the day you'll have to cry."

But why North-country women should be so persistent in their refusal to give one another a pin it is not easy to discover, for when asked for a pin they invariably reply, "You may take one, but, mind, I do not give it." This prejudice may, perhaps, have some connection with the vulgar superstition against giving a knife or any sharp instrument, as mentioned by Gay in his *Shepherd's Week* :—

> "But woe is me ! such presents luckless prove,
> For knives, they tell me, always sever love."

[1] "County Folk-lore—Suffolk." Folk-lore Society. The Lady Eveline Camilla Gurdon, 1893, p. 135.

CHAPTER IV

WOMAN'S EYES

> "Where is any author in the world
> Teaches such beauty as a woman's eye?"
>
> *Love's Labour's Lost*, act iv. sc. 3.

POETIC imagery, in painting the varied beauties of the eye, has applied to them a host of graceful and charming similes, many of which illustrate the beliefs and fancies of our forefathers respecting these so-called "keys of the human face," or, as Shakespeare has described them, "windows of the heart."

It has long been a disputed question as to what has been the recognised favourite colour of the eyes, the poets of all ages having laid much stress on the chameleon-like iris of the eye, which ever seems to vary in its green or bluish hue. Thus Homer speaks of Minerva as the "blue-eyed goddess," an epithet which has given rise to considerable comment, opinions having largely differed as to whether the poet meant this colour, or something between a green, blue, or grey.

Green eyes are often mentioned in classic literature, and they found special favour with early French poets, who were extremely fond of speaking of them under the title of *yeux vers*—a taste which seems to have been generally prevalent on the Continent. The Spaniards considered this colour of the eye an emblem of beauty, and as such there is an amusing allusion to it in "Don Quixote":—"But now I think of it, Sancho, thy description of her beauty was a little absurd in that particular of comparing her eyes to pearls. Sure, such eyes are more like those of a whiting, or a sea-bream, than those of a fair lady; and in my opinion Dulcinea's eyes are rather like two verdant emeralds, veiled in with two celestial arches, which signify her eyebrows. Therefore, Sancho, you must take your pearls from her eyes, and apply them to her teeth, for I verily believe you mistake the one for the other!" And we may quote the subjoined well-known lines in praise of green eyes, which show, like many others of the same kind, in what high esteem they were formerly held:—

"Ay ojuelos verdes,
Ay los mis ojuelos,
Ay hagan los cielos,
Qui de mi te acuerdos."

Then, again, Villa Real, a Portuguese, wrote a treatise for the purpose of setting forth the estimation in which he regarded them; and Dante, it may be remembered, speaks of Beatrice's eyes as emeralds—

> "Spare not thy vision, we have stationed thee
> Before the emeralds, whence love erewhile
> Hath drawn his weapons on thee"—

"emeralds," of course, here meaning the eyes of Beatrice.

In our own country we find no lack of allusions to green eyes, and in the "Two Noble Kinsmen" Æmilia, in her address to Diana, says: "Oh, vouchsafe with that thy rare green eye, which never yet beheld things maculate!" On the other hand, Shakespeare speaks of jealousy as "a green-eyed monster," and we know that the phrase has been frequently used in an uncomplimentary manner. But this is the exception, for what more pleasing, or graceful, instance of their being in repute as an object of beauty can be quoted than that given by Frances Collins, who tells us that her husband in writing to a certain lady always spoke of her eyes as sea-green :—

> "So stir the fire and pour the wine,
> And let those sea-green eyes divine,
> Pour their love-madness into mine."

And at another time he wrote these lines :—

> "Cupid plucked his brightest plume,
> To paint my mistress in her bloom ;
> Caught her eyes, the soft sea-green,
> At a summer noontide seen."

Longfellow in his "Spanish Student" (act ii. sc. 3) has painted with exquisite effect this phase of beauty in the following passage, where Victorian inquires: "How is that young and green-eyed Gaditana that you both wot of?" To which Don Carlos sympathetically adds, "Ay, soft, emerald eyes!" After a while, Victorian resumes her praises, remarking:—

> "You are much to blame for letting her go back.
> A pretty girl, and in her tender eyes
> Just that soft shade of green we sometimes see
> In evening skies."

But perhaps one of the highest tributes of honour to green as the colour of the eye is that given by Drummond of Hawthornden, who could not write too eulogistically of his green-eyed maiden—

> "When nature now had wonderfully wrought
> All Auristella's parts, except her eyes;
> To make those twins two lamps in beauty's skies,
> The counsel of her starry synod sought.
> Mars and Apollo first did her advise,
> To wrap in colour black those comets bright,
> That love him so might soberly disguise,
> And unperceived wound at every sight.
> Chaste Phœbe spake for purest azure dies,
> But Jove and Venus, green about the light,
> To frame thought best, as bringing most delight,
> That to pined hearts hope might for ay arise.
> Nature, all said, a paradise of green
> There placed, to make all love which have them seen."

And Mr. Swinburne in his "Félise" gives a beautiful picture of the chameleon-like iris—

"O lips that mine have grown into,
Like April's kissing May;
O fervid eyelids, letting through
Those eyes the greenest of things blue,
The bluest of things grey."

According to a writer in the *Quarterly Review*, in an amusing paper on physiognomy, the following characteristics may be ascertained by the colour of the eyes: "Dark blue eyes are most common in persons of delicate, refined, or effiminate nature; light blue, and, much more, grey eyes, in the hardy and active; greenish eyes have generally the same meaning as the grey; hazels are the more usual indications of a mind masculine, vigorous, and profound;" with which may be compared the following well-known lines:—

"Black eyes most dazzle at a ball,
Blue eyes most please at evening fall;
The black a conquest soonest gains,
The blue a conquest best retains;
The black bespeaks a lovely heart,
Whose soft emotions soon depart;
The blue a steadier frame betray,
Which burns and lives beyond a day;
The black the features best disclose,
In blue my feelings all repose;
Then each let reign without control,
The black all mind, and blue all soul."[1]

Like green, blue eyes have always been much admired, and have attracted the notice of poets. Thus Elizabeth Barrett Browning, in her "Hector in the Garden," speaks of—

"Eyes of gentianellas azure,
Staring, winking at the skies";

[1] See *Notes and Queries*, 7th, x. 471.

and Longfellow, in his "Masque of Pandora," says :—

> "O lovely eyes of azure,
> Clear as the waters of a brook that run,
> Limpid and laughing in the summer sun."

Akenside compares blue eyes to the "azure dawn," and Kirke White sings the praises of the maiden's "blue eyes' fascination." Shelley, again, in his "Prometheus Unbound," likens eyes of this colour to the "deep blue, boundless heaven ;" but it is perhaps Keats who—in his sonnet, written in answer to a sonnet by J. H. Reynolds, ending thus :—

> "Dark eyes are dearer far
> Than those that mock the hyacinthus bell"—

has given us the most elaborate picture of the charm of blue eyes :—

> "Blue ! 'tis the life of heaven—the domain
> Of Cynthia—the wide palace of the sun,
> The tent of Hesperus, and all his train,
> The bosomer of clouds, gold, grey, and dun.
> Blue ! 'tis the life of waters—Ocean
> And all its vassal streams : pools numberless
> May rage, and foam, and fret, but never can
> Subside, if not to dark-blue nativeness.
> Blue ! gentle cousin of the forest-green,
> Married to green in all the sweetest flowers,
> Forget-me-not, the Bluebell, and that Queen
> Of secrecy, the Violet : what strange powers
> Hast thou, as a mere shadow ! But how great,
> When in an Eye thou art alive with fate !" [1]

[1] Keats's Poems. Forman, vol. ii. p. 257. 1883.

There is in Spain a proverbial saying much in use which shows the high esteem in which this colour is held, and it runs thus : "Blue eyes say, 'Love me or I die' ; black eyes say, 'Love me or I kill thee' ;" and in Hindustani folk-lore a blue-eyed girl is supposed to be fortunate.

And there are numerous rhymes in this country to the same effect ; one current in Warwickshire running thus :—

"Blue-eyed—beauty,
Do your mother's duty ;
Black eye,
Brown eye,
Grey-eyed—greedy gut,
Eat all the world up."

Another version in Lincolnshire is this :—

"Blue eye—beauty.
Black eye—steal pie.
Grey eye—greedy gut.
Brown eye—love pie." [1]

Apart from blue being a much admired colour of the eye, it would seem to have gained an additional popularity from having been the recognised symbol of eternity and human immortality. Similarly the ancient heathen poets were wont to sing the praises of their "blue-eyed goddesses." Petrarch's sonnets, again, are addressed to a blue-eyed Laura. Kriemhild, of the Nibelungen Lied, is blue-eyed, like Fricka, the

[1] See Northall's "English Folk-Rhymes," p. 299.

Northern Juno, and Ingëborg of the Frithiof's Saga, and the Danish princess Iolanthe.

Blueness about the eyes, too, was considered a certain indication of love, and, to quote Lord Lytton's words, there is "a liquid melancholy of sweet eyes;" which reminds us of the simile of the Persian poet, who compares "a violet sparkling with dew" to "the blue eyes of a beautiful girl in tears;" and we may compare the remark of Rosalind to Orlando in "As You Like It" (act iii. sc. 2), who enumerates the marks of love, "a blue eye and sunken, which you have not."

Another favourite colour of the eye was grey, and Douce, in his "Illustrations of Shakespeare," quotes from the interlude of "Marie Magdalene" a song in praise of her, which says, "Your eyes as grey as glass and right amiable;" and, in the "Two Gentlemen of Verona" (act iv. sc. 4), Julia makes use of the same expression.

Black eyes have occasioned many curious fancies respecting them—some complimentary, and others just the reverse. Lord Byron, for instance, describing Leila's eyes, in the "Giacour," says:—

> "Her eye's dark charm 'twere vain to tell,
> But gaze on that of the gazelle,
> It will assist thy fancy well:
> As large, as languishingly dark,
> But soul beam'd forth in every spark."

And when addressing the maid of Athens in his tender and pathetic lines, he writes, "By those lids whose jetty fringe kiss thy soft cheeks' blooming tinge." He tells, also, how the beautiful Teresa had "the Asiatic eye" dark as the sky; and of the innocent Haidee he gives this picture :—

"Her hair, I said, was auburn, but her eyes
Were black as death, their lashes the same hue
Of downcast length, in whose silk shadows lies
Deepest attraction; for when to the view
Forth from its raven fringe the full glance flies,
Ne'er with such force the swiftest arrow flew."

Apart from poetic imagery, the black-eyed sisterhood have rarely failed to get their share of praise, although, it is true, artists have seldom, if ever, painted the Madonna dark, for, it must be remembered :—

"In the old time black was not counted fair,
Or if it were it bore not beauty's name,
But now is black beauty's successive heir."

It has been pointed out that Shakespeare only mentions black hair thrice throughout his plays. Although half, at least, of the heroines of novels are designated as having a fair complexion and the colour of the eyes that match it, we must not lose sight of the fact that the dark-eyed girl is generally supposed to be gifted with a power of force of expression which is denied to others. And as Mr. Finck remarks,[1] "Inasmuch as black-eyed Southern nations are, on the whole, more impulsive than Northern races, it may be said in a vague, general way that a black eye indicates a passionate disposition." But there are countless exceptions to this rule—as in the case of apathetic dark-eyed persons, and, conversely,

[1] "Romantic Love and Personal Beauty."

fiery, blue-eyed individuals. Nor is this at all strange, for "the black colour is not stored up in some mysterious way as a result of a fiery temperament, but is simply accumulated in the iris through natural selection as a protection against glaring sunlight."

Scottish history affords a good specimen of a dark woman in the famous "Black Agnes," the Countess of March, who was noted for her defence of Dunbar during the war with Edward III., maintained in Scotland from 1333 to the year 1338.

> "She kept astir in tower and trench,
> That brawling, boisterous, Scottish wench;
> Came I early, came I late,
> I found Black Agnes at the gate."

According to Sir Walter Scott, the Countess was called Black Agnes from her complexion. She was the daughter of Thomas Randolph, Earl of Murray. But this statement has been disputed, and it is affirmed that the lady in question was so nicknamed from the terror of her deeds, and not from her dark complexion.

The Mahometan heaven is peopled with "virgins with chaste mien and large black eyes," and we may quote what the poet of woman's lore says:—

> "The brilliant black eye
> May in triumph let fly
> All its darts without caring who feels 'em;
> But the soft eye of blue,
> Tho' it scatters wounds too,
> Is much better pleased when it heals them.

The blue eye half hid
Says from under its lid,
I love, and am yours if you love me,
The black eye may say,
Come and worship my ray,
By adoring, perhaps you may win me."

The black-eyed girl has long been credited with being deceitful, but there is little or no ground for this stigma, which, like so many other notions of a similar kind, has arisen from prejudice, or some such old adage as the following, which may be found in many parts of the country, but which, of course, is devoid of all truth :—

"Grey-eyed greedy,
Brown-eyed needy,
Black-eyed never likin',
Till it shame a' its kin."

Similar folk-rhymes are to be found in different localities, to which much faith was formerly attached by the credulous.

From a very early period various devices were employed by women for improving the colour and appearance of the eye. The ladies of the East, for instance, tinged the edges of their eyelids with the powder of lead ore, their mode of procedure being to dip into the powder a small wooden bodkin, which they drew through the eyelids over the ball of the eye. But such artificial contrivances have always proved a poor substitute for Nature's charms ; and, as Antoine Heroet, an early French poet, in his "Les Opuscules d'Amour," says of love, so it is equally true of such devices: "It is not so strange an enchanter that he can make black eyes become green, that he can turn a dark brown into clear whiteness." But, when it is remembered how enviable a prize beauty has always been, some allowance must be made for the fair sex if they have resorted to various little contrivances for enhancing the attractiveness of the most significant features of the human face.

Amongst other fancies associated with the eye we are told that "it's a good thing to have meeting eyebrows, as such a person will never know trouble;" but according to the generally considered idea such a peculiarity is far from being lucky, an illustration of which is given by Charles Kingsley in his "Two Years Ago," who thus writes: "Tom began carefully scrutinising Mrs. Harvey's face. It had been very handsome. It was still very clever, but the eyebrows clashed together downwards above her nose and rising higher at the outward corners indicated, as surely as the restless, down-drop eye, a character self-conscious, furtive, capable of great inconsistencies. possibly of great deceit." On the other hand, the Greeks admired those eyebrows which almost met, and Anacreon's mistress had this style of face:—

"Taking care her eyebrows be
Not apart, nor mingled neither,
But as hers are, stol'n together;
Met by stealth, yet leaving too
O'er the eyes their darkest hue."

Theocritus, in one of his Idylls, makes one of the speakers value himself upon the effect his beauty had on a girl with meeting eyebrows:—

> "Passing a bower last evening with my cows,
> A girl look'd out—a girl with meeting brows.
> 'Beautiful! beautiful!' cried she. I heard,
> But went on, looking down, and gave her not a word."

Chaucer apologises for Creseyde's meeting eyebrows, but Lord Tennyson's compliment of Paris to Œnone, ascribing to her "the charms of married brows," implies that they actually met. However repugnant to the modern idea of beauty meeting eyebrows may be in Europe, they are so far from being contrary to the Asiatic canon of beauty, that, where they do not exist, or where only imperfectly developed, young ladies are in the habit of prolonging the curves by means of black pigment until they are perfectly conjoined. In the same way, meeting eyebrows are much admired in Turkey, where women encourage the juncture by artificial means.

Referring to the colour of the eyebrows, it is agreed on all hands that a female eyebrow ought to be delicately and nicely pencilled. Thus Dante says of his mistress's that it looked as if it were painted—"The eyebrow, polished and dark, as though the brush had drawn it;" and Shakespeare, in his "Winter's Tale," (act ii. sc. 1) makes Mamillius speak much in the same strain:—

> "Black brows, they say,
> Become some women best, so that there be not
> Too much hair there; but in a semicircle;
> Or a half-moon made with a pen."

There can be no doubt that eyebrows have been, from time immemorial, much in request, and we know how ladies of fashion have at different times resorted to sundry expedients to give prominence to this feature of beauty. Artists have introduced them with much effect into many of their famous works of art, and poets have loved to sing of maidens with their dark eyebrows. Some, it would seem, had admired a contrast between the hair and the eyebrows, and Burns tells of a certain lass how—

> "Sae flaxen were her ringlets,
> Her eyebrows of a darker hue,
> Bewitchingly o'erarching
> Twa laughing e'en o' bonny blue."

It is curious to find how the idea of beauty, as far as the colour of the eyebrow is concerned, has undergone numerous variations. In Central Africa women stain their hair and eyebrows with indigo, and Georgian damsels, following their own idea of æsthetic taste, blacken their eyebrows, which gives them a striking appearance.

Again, Japanese ladies when married, in order to prevent any likelihood of jealousy on the part of their husbands, have long been in the habit of removing their eyebrows; and, among some of the South American and African tribes, it has been customary to eradicate or destroy the hair, a practice which has been often extended to the eyebrows and eyelashes.

Much, too, has been written on the shape of

the eyebrow, the arched one having been most generally admired. This is especially discernible in the works of the old masters, and is frequently mentioned in bygone chronicles of fashion as a distinguishing feature of many of the beautiful women of past years. But Leigh Hunt considers it doubtful whether "the eyebrows were always devised to form separate arches, or to give an arched character to the brow considered in unison." Perhaps, as he adds, a sort of double curve was recommended, "the particular one over the eye, and the general one in the look together." At any rate, a finely shaped eyebrow has rarely failed to attract attention, and as Herder has remarked, an arched eyebrow is the rainbow of peace, because when "straightened by a frown, it portends a storm."

CHAPTER V

WOMAN'S TONGUE

"How sweetly sounds the voice of a good woman!
It is so seldom heard that, when it speaks,
It ravishes all senses."

MASSINGER, *Old Law*, iv. 2.

ALTHOUGH a well-known proverb tells us that "a silent woman is always more admired than a noisy one," the Chinese have a favourite saying to the effect that "a woman's tongue is her sword, and she does not let it rust;" with which may be compared the Hindustani proverb, "For talk I'm best, for work my elder brother-in-law's wife;" which has its counterpart in this country, where it is said, "A woman's strength is in her tongue," and in Wales the adage runs thus:—

"Be she old, or be she young,
A woman's strength is in her tongue."

But proverbial literature has generally held that whatever a woman says must be received with caution; and, according to an African adage, "If a woman speaks two words take one and leave the other," with which may be compared an Eastern saying, "A woman's talk heat from grass"—that is, worthless.

But, granted the effective use frequently made by this weapon, the teachers of old were of opinion that "Silence is the best ornament of a woman;" or, as another version expresses it, "Silence is a fine jewel for a woman, but it is little worn." [1]

In days gone by a singular sign—a very favourite one with oil painters—was "The Good Woman," originally expressive of a female saint, a holy or good woman, who had met her death by the loss of her head, and how by the waggery of after ages the good woman came to be converted into the Silent Woman, as if it were a matter of necessity, is thus explained—

"A silent woman, Sir! you said;
Pray, was she painted without a head?
Yes, Sir, she was! You never read of
A silent woman with her head on.
Besides, you know, there's nought but speaking
Can keep a woman's heart from breaking!"

And M. W. Praed, in his tale of "Lillian," by an ingenious metaphor of a beautiful idiot would explain a headless woman—

"And hence the story had ever run,
That the fairest of dames was a headless one."

---

[1] See Croker's "Fairy Legends and Traditions of the South of Ireland." Edited by Thomas Wright, p. 235.

But proverbial wisdom is generally agreed that "there never was in any age such a wonder to be found as a dumb woman," and the Germans say, "when a woman has no answer the sea is empty of water."

In the old Scotch ballad of "The Dumb Wife of Aberdour," the husband is represented (writes Mr. W. A. Clouston in *Notes and Queries*, 6th Series, i. 272) as meeting with "a great grim man"—the devil, in fact—to whom he complains of his misfortune in having a wife who was dumb; upon which the Arch-fiend says to him :—

"Tak no disdain,
And I sall find remeid,
Gif thou wilt counsel keep,
And learn well what I say :
This night, in her first sleep,
Under her tongue then lay
Of quaking aspen leaf.

The whilk betokens wind,
And she shall have relief
Of speaking, thou shalt find,
What kind of tale, withouten fail,
That thou of her requires.
She shall speak out, have thou nae doubt,
And mair than thou desires."

To make sure work, the husband lays three leaves under her tongue ; and when she awoke in the morning she at once began to speak to him —with a vengeance. He afterwards consults with the fiend about making her dumb again, but quoth Satan :—

"The least devil in hell
 Can give a wife her tongue;
The greatest, I you tell,
 Can never make her dumb."

The Satanic device of placing an aspen leaf in a woman's mouth to make her speak, he adds, is alluded to in an old English book entitled "The Praise of All Women, called Mulierum Pean. Very fruitful and delectable to all the Readers—

"'Look and read who can,
This work is praise to each woman.'"

The author, Edward Gosynhill, thus accounts for the origin of woman's tongue:—

"Some say, the woman had no tongue
After that God did her create,
Until the man took leavés long
And put them under her palāte;
An aspen leaf of the devil he gat,
And for it moveth with every wind,
They say women's tongues be of like kind."

On the principle that "Speech is silver, silence is gold," it was formerly held that "One tongue is enough for two women"—an adage, we are told, which is "no less applicable to stormy Shrews than adverse to learned women who have the command of many tongues."[1] It should be remembered, also, that the rhyme, which with a slight alteration is often uttered as a warning

[1] Jeaffreson's "Brides and Bridals," vol. i. p. 350.

to children over-talking their elders, ran in former times thus :—

> "Maidens should be mild and meek,
> Swift to hear and slow to speak."

Another version slightly different is this : "Maids should be seen and not heard," which occurs in "The Maids' Complaint against the Bachelors" (1675, p. 3), where it is called "a musty proverb" ; and among further maxims, it is said, "Silence is a fine jewel for a woman but little worn," and "Silence is the best ornament of a woman."

The persistency of a woman's tongue has been made the subject of frequent comment in our proverbial lore, experience, having long proved that "a woman's tongue wags like a lamb's tail," or, as it is said in France, "Foxes are all tail, and women are all tongue." And, according to an Alsatian proverb, "If you would make a pair of good shoes, take for the sole the tongue of a woman—it never wears out." A Welsh proverb says, "Arthur could not tame a woman's tongue," which is not surprising if there be any truth in the maxim that "A woman will scold the devil out of a haunted house," which reminds us of an amusing little anecdote told of Tom Hood, who, on hearing the piety of a very loquacious lady spoken of, humorously said, "Yes, she is well known for her *mag-piety*;" and there is the German proverb, "Women are never at a loss for words." An amusing couplet, which is proverbial in the neighbourhood of Salisbury, thus speaks of a woman's tongue :—

> "Nature, regardless of the babbling race,
> Planted no beard upon a woman's face ;
> Not Freddy Keene's razors, though the very best,
> Could shave a chin that never is at rest." [1]

And as, from time immemorial, women have been accused of gossiping, it is not surprising that this fault should have been made the subject of legal penalties, as at St. Helena, where, among the ordinances promulgated in the year 1789, we find the following :—"Whereas several idle, gossiping women, made it their business to go from house to house, about this island, inventing and spreading false and scandalous reports of the good people thereof, and thereby sow discord and debate among neighbours, and often between men and their wives, to the great grief and trouble of all good and quiet people, and to the utter extinguishing of all friendship, amity, and good neighbourhood ; for the punishment and suppression thereof, and to the intent that all strife may be ended, we do order that if any women, from henceforth, shall be convicted of tale-bearing, mischief-making, scolding, or any other notorious vices, they shall be punished by ducking, or whipping, or such other punishment as their crimes or transgressions shall deserve, or the Governor and Council shall think fit."

According to an Italian saying, "three women

[1] *Notes and Queries*, 6th Series, ii. 457.

and three geese make a market," which is also found among Hindustani proverbs, "Madame Slut and two farmers' wives make a fair," a version of which has long been current in this country, where it is said, "three women make a market, four a fair," as they are sure to attract notice, and to make themselves heard. This piece of proverbial lore is alluded to in "Love's Labour's Lost' (act iii. sc. i.) :—

> "Thus came your argument in ;
> Then the boy's fat *l'envoy*, the goose that you bought."

And in an old work entitled "Marriage of Wit and Wisdom," published about the year 1570, we find the proverbial phrase, "She can cackle like a cadowe," *i.e.*, a jackdaw, with which may be compared the adage, "She's a wagtail." An early MS. of the fifteenth century contains this version :

> "A young wife and a harvest goose,
> Much cackle will both ;
> A man that hath them in his clos [possession],
> He shall rest wroth."

And we may compare with the above the following from the old nursery rhyme :—

> "Misses One, Two, and Three, could never agree,
> While they gossiped round a tea-caddy."

A woman's tongue, again, it is said, must not be always trusted, for "a honey tongue, a heart of gall," or, as another version puts it, "Too much courtesy, too much craft." Similarly, an African proverb says, "Trust not a woman, she will tell thee what she has just told her companion;" and a Turkish adage tells us not to "trust the promise of the great, the calm of the sea, the evening twilight, the word of a woman, or the courage of the horse." Nothing, too, is more derogatory to a woman than coarse or bad language, and hence she is warned that "Bad words make a woman worse:" words which call to mind Martial's epigram :—

"Fair, rich, and young! How rare is her perfection,
Were it not mingled with one foul infection;
So proud a heart, so cursed a tongue,
As makes her seem nor rich, nor fair, nor young."

And a popular maxim attributed to Tasso tells us that "Women have tongues of craft, and hearts of guile;" and, on this account, we are told that "he who listens to the words of a woman will be accounted worthless," as, not only lacking common sense, but as acting on her advice which can bring him no good.

Although proverbial wisdom is agreed that, to quote a German adage, "A woman has never spoiled anything through silence," her fondness of talking is further exemplified in such proverbs as "Her tongue steals away all the time from her hands," and "All women are good Lutherans," they say in Denmark, "because they would rather preach than hear Mass;" whereas the old English saying enjoins, "Let women spin and not preach." One of Heywood's proverbs tells us that "Husbands are in heaven whose wives scold not," which is similar to the well-known adage :—

"It is a good horse that never stumbles,
And a good wife that never grumbles ;"

for, as it is commonly said throughout Scotland, "A house wi' a reek and a wife with a reerd will make a man rin to the door," a dictum which has its equivalent in Spain—

"Smoke, a dripping roof, and a scolding wife,
Are enough to drive a man out of his life."

a version of which was formerly current in the North of England :—

"Smoke, rain, and a very curst wife,
Make a man weary of house and life ;"

and we may compare the Hindustani proverb which, describing a woman who is quarrelsome beyond endurance, says, "She quarrels with the breeze." Disagreeable as such tongues may be, equally to be avoided is "a groaning wife," for as the Scotch peasantry tell us, "a grunting horse and a graneing wife seldom fail their master," implying that women who are constantly in the habit of complaining how ill they are, generally contrive to live as long as their neighbours.

Closely allied with the proverbial lore associated with a woman's tongue may be mentioned the strong antipathy to a woman whistling about a house or even out of doors, for, according to a well-known proverb, of which there are several versions :—

> "A whistling woman and a crowing hen,
> Are neither fit for God nor men;"

or, as they say in the West of England, "A whistling woman and a crowing hen are two of the unluckiest things under the sun." Why there should be this deep-rooted prejudice it is difficult to decide, unless we accept the explanation in the subjoined couplet :—

> "A whistling wife and a crowing hen,
> Will call the old gentleman out of his den;"

or, as the peasantry say in Cheshire, "Will fear the old lad out of his den." There are numerous versions of this popular piece of folk-lore, one warning us that—

> "Whistling girls and crowing hens,
> Always come to some bad end;"

and again—

> "A whistling wife and a crowing hen,
> Will come to God, but God knows when;"

and we may compare the Sinhalese proverb, "It is said that even the hen reared by a talkative woman crows." This superstition, too, is largely shared by the seafaring community, and, some years ago when a party of ladies were going on board a vessel at Scarborough, the captain declined to allow one to enter, exclaiming, "Not that young lady, she whistles." Curiously enough the vessel was wrecked on her next voyage, so had the young lady set foot on it, the catastrophe would have been attributed to her. A correspondent of *Notes and Queries* tells us that, one day after trying to induce his dog to come into the house, his wife essayed to whistle, when she was suddenly interrupted by a servant—a Roman Catholic—who apologetically said, "If you please, ma'am, don't whistle. Every time a woman whistles, the heart of the Blessed Virgin bleeds." Another legend informs us that the superstition originated in the circumstance that a woman stood by and whistled as she watched the nails for the cross being forged. The French have a similar prejudice, their proverb running as follows :—"Une poule qui chante le coq, et une fille qui jiffle, portent malheur dans la maison," a variation of which runs thus :—

"La maison est misérable et méchante
Ou la poule plus haut que le coq chant."

("That house doth everday more wretched grow,
Where the hen louder than the cock doth crow");

and another popular adage warns us that—

"La poule ne doit pas chanter devant le coq,"

a translation of which is sometimes heard in our own country :—

"Ill fares the hapless family that shows,
A cock that's silent, and a hen that crows."

This superstition, too, is not confined to Europe, for there is a Chinese proverb to the same effect :—

> "A bustling woman and crowing hen,
> Are neither fit for gods nor men."

It is an injunction of the priesthood, writes a correspondent of *Notes and Queries* (4th Series, xi. 475), "and a carefully observed household custom, to kill immediately every hen that crows, as a preventive against the misfortune which the circumstance is supposed to indicate;" and the same practice, he adds, prevails throughout many parts of the United States. The Japanese tells us that "when the hen crows the house goes to ruin," with which may be compared the Russian adage, "It never goes well when the hen crows," whilst the Persian proverb puts the matter sensibly thus: —"If you be a cock, crow; if a hen, lay eggs;" and there is the Portuguese maxim with a similar meaning, "It is a silly flock where the ewe bears the bell;" a further proverb telling us that "a house is in a bad case where the distaff commands the sword;" and the Italians go still further, for they say that "when a woman reigns the devil frowns," to which may be added the Indian adage, "What trust is there in a crowing hen?"

From the numerous instances recorded of this piece of folk-lore we may quote an amusing extract from one of Walpole's letters to Lady Ossory, January 8, 1772, wherein after informing her Ladyship of the damage done to his castle by the explosion of the Hounslow Powder Mills, he humorously writes :—

"Margaret [his housekeeper] sits by the waters of Babylon and weeps over Jerusalem. Yet she was not taken quite unprepared, for one of the Bantam hens had crowed on Sunday morning, and the chandler's wife told her three weeks ago, when the Barn was blown down, that ill-luck never came single. She is, however, very thankful that the china-room has escaped, and says God has always been the best creature in the world to her."

But a talkative, as well as a whistling, woman is, in German lore, equally warned against making an undue use of her tongue, for "a glaring sunny morning, a woman that talks Latin, and a child reared on wine never come to a good end ;" or, as another adage has it, "A woman and a hen are soon lost in gadding" ; and according to another warning, whereas "a gossiping woman talks of every one, every one talks of her."[1] The most remarkable thing, as the Japanese say, is that, although "a woman's tongue is only three inches long, it can kill a man six feet high ;" but the Chinese have a common proverb to the effect that, whereas "a man's words are like an arrow close to the mark, a woman's is like a broken fan." A further way, also, in which woman is occasionally able to use her tongue to advantage is in the art of dissimulation when love is concerned, a piece

[1] See J. Barten's "Collection of English and German Proverbs," Hamburg, 1890.

of craft which, skilfully devised, has deceived many a lover, for, as the Spanish adage goes—

> "He that speaks me fair and loves me not,
> I'll speak him fair and love him not;"

with which may be compared the Hindustani proverb, "A shrill tongue and a false hand."

But, after all, it must not be forgotten that even "the whisper of a beautiful woman can be heard further than the loudest call of duty;" and again, "A sweet tongue will conquer the whole world, and a crooked one will estrange it."

CHAPTER VI

WOMAN'S GOODNESS

"And whether coldness, pride, or virtue dignify
A woman, so's she's good what does it signify!"
BYRON, *Don Juan*.

IF we are to believe an old German proverb, "there are only two good women in the world: one of them is dead, and the other is not to be found"—a statement which probably even few disparagers of the fair sex would be ready to accept, although it may be supplemented by an equally ungallant French saying which asserts that "a man of straw is worth a woman of gold."

But it must be remembered that, in formulating maxims of this kind, individual prejudice has in only too many cases been responsible for originating them, and, despite their having in the course of years passed into proverbs, they must not always be regarded as expressive of the consensus of opinion of the country to which they belong.

Thus, going back to an early period, Ovid was of opinion that "it is easy for a woman to be good when all that hinders her from being so is removed;" and, although an old English proverb says, "All women are good," it qualifies this assertion by cautiously adding, "good for something, or good for nothing;" but the Hindu proverb declares that "oil and the pure woman will both rise."

With all due deference to the fair sex, it must unfortunately be acknowledged that much of the proverbial lore under this heading relating to them is far from being of a complimentary nature, as who, for instance, has not heard of the familiar adage:—

> "If a woman were as little as she is good,
> A peascod would make her a gown and a hood;"

and, "She's a good maid, but for thought, word, and deed." And this estimate of woman's worth has been largely endorsed by those who have generally been credited with having possessed some knowledge of human life. Thus Pope says:—

> "Shouldst thou search the spacious world around,
> Yet one good woman is not to be found;"

and Massinger speaks in the same strain:—

> "How sweetly sounds the voice of a good woman.
> It is so seldom heard that, when it speaks,
> It ravishes all senses."

But, confining ourselves more especially to the proverbial lore of the subject, the Spanish warn a man to "beware of a bad woman, and to put no trust in a good one;" and according to an African proverb, "a woman never brings a man into the right way." Plautus, too, was of the same opinion, remarking, "He that can avoid women, let him do so, so as to take care each day not to do what he may regret on the morrow."

The scarcity of good women is often illustrated by such adages as the following :—

> "A good woman is worth—if she were sold—
> The fairest crown that's made of pure gold"

—the idea, of course, being that such a woman is not to be found; with which may be compared the couplet :—

> "Show me a man without a spot,
> And I'll show you a maid without a blot."

Again, the familiar couplet :—

> "A spaniel, a woman, and a walnut tree,
> The more they're beaten the better they be,"

may be traced back as far as Martial. There are several versions of this time-honoured maxim, one of which is furnished by Moor in his "Suffolk Words" (p. 465) :—

> "Three things by beating better prove—
> A nut, an ass, a woman:
> The cudgel from their back remove,
> And they'll be good for no man."

Webster, in his "White Devil" (1612, act iv. sc. 4), had the same proverb in mind when he made Flamineo say:—

> "Why do you kick her, say?
> Do you think that she's like a walnut tree?
> Must she be cudgell'd ere she bear good fruit?"

And at the present day the Italians are wont to affirm, "Women, asses, and nuts require rough hands;" with which may be compared the Chinese adage, "Nothing will frighten a wilful wife but a beating." Such chastisement of women was really carried into effect in the so-called days of chivalry, as may be inferred from the precepts of the knightly orders which directed that ladies should be treated respectfully and tenderly. And yet, on the other hand, as it has been pointed out, "the social annals of our Anglo-Saxon period comprise revolting stories of the barbarity of mistresses to their slaves; and in later times the lady of a castle or manorial seat was accustomed to rule her children and domestics with a severity surpassing that of the lord whom she obeyed with fear." But happily woman no longer lives under the lash as in the days of long ago, and, no matter how bad her character may be—

> "The man who lays his hand upon a woman,
> Save in the way of kindness, is a wretch,
> Whom 'twere gross flattery to name a coward."

Indeed, he would be a bold man who, nowadays, would think to follow out with impunity the spirit of the old proverbial philosophy, and, under the impression that he was making his wife a good woman, put into practice the following admonition :—

> "The crab of the wood is sauce very good
> For the crab of the sea ;
> But the wood of the crab is sauce for a drab
> That will not her husband obey."

The same idea is embodied in numerous other items of proverbial lore, such as "A ship and a woman want always trimming ;" or, as another version has it, "Women are ships and must be manned." But this apparently does not always answer, for, as an old folk-rhyme reminds us :—

> "To talk well with some women doth as much good
> As a sick man to eat up a load of greenwood."

And, *à propos* of the subject, we may quote the case of the young girl who, on receiving an offer of marriage which she wished to accept, submitted the matter to her father, who advised her against matrimony, using as an argument St. Paul's words, "They who marry do well ; but they who do not, do better." "Well," replied the damsel, "I love to do well ; let those do better who can."

The Scotch would appear to be more gallant in their opinion of the fair sex, if we can place reliance on the following adage :—

> "A' are gude lasses, but where do the ill wives come frae ?"

—a saying which has its equivalent in Spain, where there is a proverb, "All are good maids, but whence come the bad wives ?"

Even the good woman is warned against the contaminating influence of her own sex, for, as an Eastern piece of proverbial lore tells us, "A good woman, beset by evil women, is like the chaste mimosa surrounded by poisonous herbs"—illustrations of which maxim under a variety of forms are to be met with in most countries; [1] a popular Oriental adage warning us that "bad company is friendship with a snake fencing with a sword." But it has been generally held that "as the woman, so her friends," an Osmandi proverb reminding us that "the life of a good woman is shown by her companions."

Equivocal as many of the proverbial sayings are when speaking of woman's goodness, it may be noted that the reverse is invariably the case in the folk-tales and legends which have immortalised in a hundred and one ways their deeds of bravery and self-denial. At Lilliard's Edge, for instance, in Roxburghshire, was fought, in 1545, the battle of Ancrum Moor, in which, according to tradition, a female warrior named Lilliard, when covered with wounds, continued to fight on the Scotch side, in the name of Squire Witherington. Buried on the field of victory, a stone was raised to her good memory, on which were written these words:—

"Fair Maiden Lilliard lies under the stane,
Little was her stature, but great was her fame;
Upon the English loons she laid mony thumps,
And when her legs were cuttit off, she fought upon her stumps."

[1] Rev. J. Long's "Eastern Proverbs and Emblems," 1881, p. 25.

Folk-lore can boast of numerous historic rhymes of this class, and elsewhere we have alluded to some of the old Church builder's legends which owe their origin to the marvellous efforts of noble and good women. Thus, to give one example, a pretty legend is told of the building of Linton Church, which is situated on a little knoll of fine, compact sand, without any admixture of stone, even pebbles, and widely different from the soil of the neighbouring heights. The sand has, however, hardened into stone, yet the particles are so coherent that the sides of ready-made graves appear smooth as a wall to the depth of fifteen feet. This singular phenomenon is thus accounted for by the local tradition: Many, many years ago a young man killed a priest, and was condemned to death for murder and sacrilege. By the intervention of two good women—his two sisters—his life was spared on condition that they should sift as much sand as would form a mound on which to build a church.

The maidens undertook the task, but on their brother's liberation at the completion of the church one of them died immediately "either from the effects of past fatigue, or overpowering joy." [1]

[1] See Henderson's "Folk-lore of the Northern Counties."

CHAPTER VII

BAD WOMEN

"A worthless woman! Mere cold clay
As false things are! but so fair,
She takes the breath of man away
Who gaze upon her unaware."

E. B. Browning,
Bianca among the Nightingales.

ACCORDING to the trite old adage, "Man, woman, and the devil are the three degrees of comparison," for it has long been agreed that when a woman is bad she far excels man in evil, a maxim which has been upheld by the proverb lore of most countries; a Chinese proverb affirming that "there is no such poison in the green snake's mouth, or the hornet's sting, as in a woman's heart;" and the Italians say that "it is better to irritate a dog than a bad woman," which is similar to the German saying, "An ill-tempered woman is the devil's door-nail." According to a familiar adage:—

"A wicked woman and an evil
Is three-halfpence worse than the devil,"

which is to the same effect as the oft-quoted proverb, "A woman and her servant, acting in accord, would outwit a dozen devils;" or, as another version has it, "A woman is some nine points worse than than the devil," being much to the same purport as the Italian proverb, "Women know a point more than the devil;" and to Congreve's adaptation of Ovid's lines:—

> "Would you increase the craft of womankind,
> Teach them new wiles and arts? As well you may
> Instruct a snake to bite or wolf to prey;"

all of which may be supplemented by Victor Hugo's words, "Men are women's playthings, women are the devil's;" for as our own proverb says, "She-devils are hard to turn."

In the "Hitopadesa,"—one of the choice treasure-houses of Sanskrit wisdom—it is declared that, "Infidelity, violence, deceit, envy, extreme avariciousness, a total want of qualities, with impurity, are the innate faults of womankind;" with which may be compared Goëthe's views, "When we speed to the devil's house woman takes the lead by a thousand steps;" and there is a Sinhalese adage, "If you want to go to the gallows without the aid of a ladder, you can go by the aid of a woman."

There is a proverbial saying in Leicestershire, "Shay's as nasty as a devil unknobbed," *i.e.*, a devil who has either never had any knobs fastened on his horns, or else has succeeded in getting rid of them; the phrase illustrating the bovine character of the popular devil;[1] all of which statements recall the passage in Beaumont and Fletcher's comedy of Monsieur Thomas (act iii. sc. 1):—

> "Oh, woman, perfect woman! what distraction
> Was meant to mankind when thou wast made a devil!
> What an inviting hell invented."

According to Hindustani proverbial lore, "the elder sister-in-law is the devil's wand, when you see her she stands as straight as an arrow," the meaning being that she is the chief disturber of the family peace; and by a well-known Oriental adage a very bad woman is spoken of as "the devil's aunt." Marathi proverbial wisdom says that in one fair woman there are seventy-two hidden vices," and that when she has had her fill of wickedness she takes to religion, and we may quote the Sindhi proverb, "Women, land, and money are all three homes of death"—in other words, they are the causes of many murders. An old Latin proverb goes so far as to say that "when a woman is openly bad she is then at her best;" another one illustrating the same idea in a different wording, "A wicked woman is a magazine of evils." It is further said that "it is better to dwell with a dragon than with a wicked woman;" and there is some truth in this warning if the subjoined couplet be correct:—

> "For woman's soul when once plunged in
> Knows no stopping place in sin."

[1] A. B. Evans, "Leicestershire Words, Phrases, and Proverbs," 1881, p. 282.

Alexander Dumas puts into the mouth of an officer of the Paris detective force the well-known expression, "*Cherchez la femme*"—"Search for the women"—which corresponds with our saying, "Wherever there is anything wrong there is generally a woman in the case," or as Richardson says, "A plot must have a woman in it." Sardou, it may be remembered, introduces the phrase in his drama "Ferréol;" and George Ebers ("Uarda," vol. ii. cap. 14) says:—

> "You forget that there is a woman in this.
> That is so all the world over, replied Ameni."

Sometimes the expression takes the form of, "*Où est la femme?*"—"Where is the woman? Where is she? What is her name?"

Again, it is said, "Women are saints in the church, angels in the street, devils in the kitchen, and apes in bed," a saying which, says Hazlitt, "is rather elaborately illustrated in Jacques Olivier's work entitled 'L'Alphabet de l'Imperfection des Femmes,' which was first published about the year 1617;" and which reminds us of the adage, "Women are demons who make us enter hell through the gates of Paradise." There are many proverbs to the same purport, some of which are couched in stronger language than others. Thus one much used, in days gone by, amongst the peasantry throughout the country says:—

> "A woman that is wilful is a plague of the worst;
> As well live in hell as with a wit that is curst."

And, owing to the fact that the fair sex have from the earliest period been regarded as mischievous, we find them styled "the devil's tools" and "the devil's nets"—a host of other uncomplimentary epithets having been applied to them for which, it must be acknowledged, there is little or no warranty. Pope says, "Every woman is at heart a rake," and Lord Lytton in his "Lady of Lyons":—

> "Thou art the author
> Of such a book of follies in a man,
> That it would need the tears of all the angels,
> To blot the record out!"

with which may be compared the popular saying, "When a woman thinks by herself she thinks of evil," and with the Italian saying, "It is vain to watch a really bad woman." There can be no doubt, however, that in many of the allusions of this kind relating to women justice has not been done to them, and there is some reason in the proverb of the Italian sisterhood, "In men every mortal sin is venial; in women every venial sin is mortal."

Amongst some of the bad qualities condemned in women, and against which man is warned in our proverbial literature, may be mentioned intemperance, and loose morals. According to one folk-rhyme—

> "Women and wine, game, and deceit,
> Make the wealth small, and the wants great"—

which is told in various ways. In an old manuscript of the fifteenth century five evils to be avoided are thus summed up :—

> " A young man a ruler, reckless ;
> An old man a lecher, loveless ;
> A poor man a waster, good-less ;
> A rich man a thief, needless ;
> A woman a ribald, shameless :
> These five shall never thrive blameless."

Another version evidently of this old proverbial maxim communicated to *Current Notes* for December, 1853, runs thus :—

> " A wife that is unchaste is like a filthy sow ;
> An old man a lecher nothing more to be hated ;
> A woman unshamefast, a child unchastised,
> Is worse than gall, where poison is undesired."

Similarly one ot Heywood's proverbs tells us how—

> " Gaming, women, and wine,
> While they laugh, they make men pine ; "

with which may be compared the adage, " Play, women, and wine undo men laughing ; " or, as another version has it, " Women, money, and wine, have their good and their pine." But the illustrations already given show that some of the most severe strictures passed on women are those which relate to unchastity, one or two further instances of which we subjoin :—

> " An unchaste wife, working mischief still,
> Is oft compared to a foul dunghill."

And—

> "A woman that spins in vice
> Has her smock full of lice."

Again, we are told that "A fair woman without virtue is like palled wine;" an Arabian version being, "An immodest woman is food without bait;" or, as it is thus said in some country villages, "A fair woman with foul conditions is like a sumptuous sepulchre, full of corruption;" and further, "She that loseth her modesty and honesty hath nothing else worth losing;" reminding us of the warning often given to those about to get married, "A fair face may be a foul bargain," inasmuch as—

> "There cannot be a greater clog to man,
> Than to be weary of a wanton woman."

The Scotch say, "Ye may drive the deil into a wife, but ye'll ne'er ding him oot o' her," implying that when a woman is once bad there is no chance of reclaiming her; and hence we cannot be surprised at the German proverb, "A bag of fleas is easier to keep guard over than a woman."

But, whether we regard women as good or bad, it is generally agreed they surpass man in either case, for, as the French say, "Women, ever in extremes, are always either better or worse than men," with which may be compared the following lines in Lord Tennyson's "Idylls," "Merlin and Vivien":—

> "For men at most differ as Heaven and Earth,
> But women, worst and best, as Heaven and Hell."

Occasionally old local rhymes allude in somewhat uncomplimentary language to the bad qualities of the fair sex. The island of Iona is separated from Mull by a strait about a mile long. An islet close to the Mull shore opposite the ruins of Iona is designated "The Woman's Island," owing to a tradition of Columba that he would not allow a woman or a cow to remain on his own island. The reason assigned for this ungracious command is embodied in an old folk-rhyme:—

"Where there is a cow,
There will be a woman;
And where there is a woman,
There will be mischief"—

a saying which, we are told, is in certain parts of Scotland repeated as a good-humoured satire on women.

It has long been admitted, even by those who disparage women's virtues, that her memory is excellent when she is anxious to keep anything in mind, and hence it is said that "if a woman has any malicious mischief to do her memory is immortal." Proverbial wisdom, again, tells how worthless and unprincipled women often amuse themselves by dissimulation, even going so far as to feign love: an apt illustration of such sham love from Hindustani proverb runs thus, "I'll love him and I'll caress him and I'll put fire under him; if it burn him what can I do?"[1] and there is a well-known Arabic adage which warns us that, "Women's immorality and monks' wiles are to be dreaded."

[1] See Fallon's "Hindustani Proverbs."

CHAPTER VIII

WOMAN'S LOVE

"There is no paradise on earth equal to the union of love and innocence."—ROUSSEAU.

ACCORDING to Lord Byron, "Man's love is of man's life a thing apart; 'tis woman's whole existence;" and under a thousand images the poets of all ages have depicted her as a mysterious mixture of joy and sadness, of agony and delight. But the truth of the well-known apothegm cannot be denied, "'Tis love, 'tis love that makes the world go round," for :—

"Love rules the court, the camp, the grove,
And men below and saints above;
For love is heaven, and heaven is love."

It is only natural that much should have been written on woman's love—that inexhaustible theme which will continue to hold its sway till the end of time; for, as it was long ago said, "A woman will dare anything when she loves or hates." And yet, strange to say, it must be acknowledged the love of woman has always been more or less enigmatical in the eyes of man, on account of its only too often eccentric and contradictory nature. Thus Middleton speaks of love's strange antics :—

"Love is ever sick, and yet is never dying,
Love is ever true, and yet is ever lying ;
Love does doat in liking, and is mad in loathing :
Love, indeed, is anything ; yet, indeed, is nothing."

Southwell describes a woman's loving looks as "murdering darts," and elsewhere he says :—

"She offereth joy, but bringeth grief,
A kiss—where she doth kill."

The hesitancy with which a woman furtively, and oftentimes playfully, tries to conceal her love by a slight cough, has from an early period been humorously recognised in proverbial love, as in the old adage, "Love and a cough cannot be hid," the Latin equivalent of which is, "Amor tussis que non celantur," versions of which are to be met with in French and Italian proverbs.[1] Similarly we may compare the proverb :—

"When a musician hath forgot his note,
He makes as though a crumb stuck in his throat."

Thackeray has described "the delights and tortures, the jealousy and wakefulness, the longing and raptures, the frantic despair and elation,

[1] See Hazlitt's "English Proverbs," 1869, p. 269.

attendant upon the passion of love;" and, indeed, volumes might be written illustrative of the mysterious workings of woman's love, although Alphonse Karr went so far as to affirm: "Women for the most part do not love us. They do not choose a man because they love him, but because it pleases them to be loved by him." But, whatever may have been written descriptive of love, its influence is indisputable, and as the Scotch say, "Love is as warm amang cottars as courtiers;" and, as it has been truly said:—

> "The rose blooms gay on shairney brae,
> As weel's in briken shaw;
> And love will lowe in cottage low,
> As weel's in lofty ha';"

with which may be compared the English equivalent, "Love lives in cottages as well as in courts."

Proverbial literature naturally has much to say on the power of a woman's love, and, according to a popular French adage, "Love subdues all but the ruffian's heart;" and history abounds in illustrations of this maxim, which under a variety of forms is found all over the world, one of the best-known versions being, "Love rules his kingdom without a sword."

And yet it is agreed that woman's love is only too frequently far from kind, for, as it was proverbially said by our forefathers, "Love is a sweet tyranny, because the lover endureth his torments willingly." The French have a proverb to the same effect: "He who has love in his heart has spurs in his sides," the chief reason for this being the anxiety of the fair sex to show their mastery over man ; for, like St. Augustine, they have always been of opinion that "he that is not jealous is not in love." Hence a woman is fond of testing her lover's faith by kindling his jealousy, adhering to the time-honoured proverb, "There is no love without jealousy." On the other hand, we are told that "Love expels jealousy," and, according to an Italian belief, "It is better to have a husband without love than with jealousy," which calls to mind Iago's words ("Othello," act iii. sc. 3) :—

> "O, beware, my lord, of jealousy,
> It is the green-eyed monster which doth mock
> The meat it feeds on."

But jealousy is not confined to either sex, for—

> "The venom clamours of a jealous woman
> Poison more deadly than a mad dog's tooth."

But it is generally agreed that there is nothing worse than a jealous woman, and a piece of African proverbial wisdom tells us that "a jealous woman has no flesh upon her breast ; for, however much she may feed upon jealousy, she will never have enough."

And yet, although French romance is full of the tortures which lovers have experienced from the fair sex, it is said :—

> "Amour, tous les autres plaisirs
> Ne valent pas tes peines,"

which has been translated thus: "O Love, thy pains are worth more than all other pleasures"—a statement which is much open to doubt.

Again, woman's love when it "comes apace" is to be avoided as untrustworthy and likely as suddenly to wane; on which account it is commonly said, "Hasty love is iron hot and iron cold." In "Ralph Roister Doister," written about the year 1550, Christian Custance says: "Gay love, God save it! So soon hot, so soon cold." But the love which lasts is that recommended in one of Heywood's proverbs, "Love me little, love me long," which Hazlitt mentions as the title of an old ballad licensed to W. Griffith in 1569–1570.

Woman's love has ever been open to reproach as being fickle and unstable, and Southey, quoting the popular sentiment, says:—

> "There are three things a wise man will not trust,
> The wind, the sunshine of an April day,
> And woman's plighted faith;"

further instances of which trait of character will be found elsewhere, where we have dealt with the fickleness of the fair sex. But the swain who is disheartened by his lady-love's coquetry, and is afraid of losing her through excessive wooing, folk-lore admonishes him thus:—

> "Follow love and it will flee;
> Flee love, and it will follow thee."

Indeed satirists have long since told us, in most countries, the folly of believing in a woman's expression of love, as "the last suitor wins the maid"—an adage which has also been expressed in this proverbial couplet:—

> "The love of a woman and a bottle of wine,
> Are sweet for a season and last for a time."

and it has been suggested that it was owing to woman's fickleness that the saying originated, "Happy is the wooing that is not long in doing"—the prudent man thereby not giving her the opportunity of changing her mind.

But fickle and unstable as a woman's love probably may be, there is no gainsaying its power, and in China it is said of a woman who captivates a man, "With one smile she overthrows a city; with another a kingdom." According to the popular tradition this proverb originated in the following circumstance:—A certain lady named Hsi-Shih, the concubine of Fu Cha, King of the ancient State of Wu. She was eminently beautiful, and her beauty so captivated her lord that for her sake he neglected the affairs of his kingdom, which in consequence fell into disorder and ruin.

Whatever the value either of a woman's love or beauty, the folk-tales of most countries agree in one respect—the exacting conditions demanded of the suitor, as a price for gaining his heart's desire, although, under a variety of forms, the subjoined couplet is no doubt founded on the experience of womanhood:—

> "Lads' love is lassies' delight,
> And if lads don't love, lasses will flite [*scold*]."

And yet, according to a common piece of West African wisdom, "If thou givest thy heart to a woman she will kill thee." Wanting in chivalry, as many such proverbs are, there is one current in China, the truth and wisdom of which most persons will endorse: "Where true love exists between husbands and wives, they're happily joined to the end of their lives."

CHAPTER IX

WOMAN'S HATE

"Not even the soldiers' fury, raised in war,
The rage of tyrants when defiance stings 'em!
The pride of priests, so bloodless when in power,
Are half so dreadful as a woman's vengeance."

SAVAGE.

IT is generally agreed that a thing to be avoided by man at any cost is a woman's hatred; although, according to Walter Savage Landor, "No friendship is so cordial or so sweet as that of a girl for a girl; no hatred so intense or immovable as that of woman for woman." And the dislike of one woman for another is mostly attributed to jealousy; for, according to a common French proverb, "It is the men who cause the women to dislike each other."

But, as it has been observed, "The anger of a woman is the greatest evil with which one can threaten enemies, especially as proverbial experience tells us that "A woman is more constant in hate than in love;" a maxim which has additional warning when it is remembered that "No woman is too silly not to have a genius for spite"—added to which may be quoted this piece of German proverb lore: "A woman's vengeance knows no bounds;" and, again: "A woman, when inflamed by love or hatred, will do anything." To the same effect is the French saying: "Women's counsels are ever cruel," the warning being added that "you should believe only one word in forty that a woman speaks," a fact which is said to be specially true when she is anxious to emphasise her expressions of hatred against her unfortunate victim.

And we are reminded that the hate of a woman is all the more to be dreaded, for even when at her best we are told that "Women like good wine are a secret poison," and that "whereas women's love is dangerous, their hate is fatal."

This view, too, is the same everywhere, and a well-known Hindustani maxim tells us that "the rage of a woman, a player, and a bull is something dreadful;" but it consoles us by adding that "A woman's threats and goblin's stones break no bones."

And, as in love, so in hate, a woman is mentally proverbially blind, seeing nothing but what is thoroughly bad in the object of her hatred; and hence the popular proverb, of which there are many versions: "Hatred is blind as well as love."

CHAPTER X

LOVE TESTS

"'Twas the maiden's matchless beauty
That drew my heart a-nigh;
Not the fern-root potion,
But the glance in her blue eye."

IT has been remarked that one of the grandest musical works in existence would never have been written had not Tristram and Ysonde drank the magic potion, which was so strong that it united them even after death; for from his grave there grew an eglantine, which twined about Ysonde's statue above, and, though three times they cut it down, it grew again, and ever wound its arms round the image of the fair Ysonde.

As a means of inspiring and securing love, amatory potions and love charms of all kinds have been much in request amongst the fair sex; and even, at the present day, cases occur now and again of persons being fined for either selling, or persuading lovesick damsels to purchase, various mysterious compounds for influencing the affections of others. Going back to early times, it is well known that the Roman poet Lucretius took his life in an amorous fit caused by a love potion, and Lucullus lost his reason in the same way. In the Middle Ages love-powders were advertised for sale, the pernicious effects of which became a matter of serious comment.

Shakespeare has represented Othello as winning Desdemona by such means:—

> "She is abused, stolen from me, and corrupted
> By spells of medicines bought of mountebanks."

Formerly the village apothecary kept love-philtres among his stock of drugs; and Gay, in his "Shepherds' Week," tells how Hobnelia was guilty of resorting to this questionable practice:—

> "As I was wont, I trudged, last market-day,
> To town with new-laid eggs, preserved in hay;
> I made my market long before 'twas night,
> My purse grew heavy, and my basket light.
> Straight to the 'pothecary shop I went,
> And in love-powder all my money spent.
> Behap what will, next Sunday, after prayers,
> When to the ale-house Lubberkin repairs,
> These golden flies into his mug I'll throw,
> And soon the swain with fervent love shall glow."

Similarly, in the "Character of a Quack Astrologer," published in the year 1673, we are told how "He induces a young heiress to run away with a footman by persuading a young girl 'tis her destiny, and sells the old and ugly philtres and love-powder to procure them sweethearts."

In the preparation of the love-philtre, much

importance has been attached to the ingredients used in its composition, certain plants and animals having been supposed to be specially adapted for such a purpose. Italian girls, for instance, still practise the following method: A lizard is caught, drowned in wine, dried in the sun, and reduced to powder, some of which is thrown on the obdurate man, who thenceforth is hers for evermore. A favourite Slavonic device with a lovesick girl, writes Mr. Finck, in his "Romantic Love and Personal Beauty," "is to cut the finger, let a few drops of her blood run into a glass of beer, and make the adored man drink it unknowingly. The same method is current in Hesse and Oldenburg; and in Bohemia, the girl who is afraid to wound her finger may substitute a few drops of bat's blood."

Another form of this mode of procedure practised by girls on the Continent is this: "Take a holy wafer, but which has not yet been consecrated, write on it certain words from the ring-finger, and then let a priest say five masses over it; divide the wafer into two equal parts, of which keep one, and give the other to the person whose love you desire to gain."

Flowers have been much in request as love-philtres, a favourite one having been the pansy. Oberon tells Puck to place a pansy on the eyes of Titania in order that on awaking she may fall in love with the first object she meets:—

> "Fetch me that flower—the herb I showed thee once;
> The juice of it on sleeping eyelids laid
> Will make a man, or woman, madly dote
> Upon the next live creature that it sees."

Vervain has long been in repute as a love-producer, and in many rural districts has the reputation amongst the fair sex of securing affection from those who take it to those who administer it. Another ingredient of the amatory potion once highly prized was cumin-seed. It is still popular with country lasses in Italy, who endeavour to make their sweethearts swallow it in order to insure their continued attachment and fidelity. Or if the lover is going to serve as a soldier, or has obtained employment in a distant part of the country, his lady-love gives him a newly-made loaf seasoned with cumin, or some wine in which cumin has been previously powdered and mixed.

Another mystic plant is the basil, which in Moldavia is said to stop the wandering youth on his way, and to make him love the maiden from whose hand he happens to accept a sprig. Indeed, rarely does the Italian girl pay a visit to her sweetheart without wearing behind her ear a sprig of this favourite plant. The mandrake, which is still worn in France as a love-charm, was formerly in demand by English girls for the same purpose, because, writes Gerarde, "It hath been thought that the root hereof serveth to win love." He also speaks of the carrot as "Serving for love matters," and adds that the root of the wild species is more effectual than that of the garden.

The root of the male-fern was, in days gone by, much sought for in the preparation of love-philtres, and hence the following allusion:—

"'Twas the maiden's matchless beauty
That drew my heart a-nigh;
Not the fern-rood potion,
But the glance of her blue eye."

With Indian women the mango is a favourite plant in love matters. Tradition tells how once upon a time a young girl plucked one of its blossoms, and offered it to Cupid, uttering these words:—

"God of the bow, who with spring's choicest flowers
Dost point the five unerring shafts; to thee
I dedicate this blossom; let it serve
To barb thy truest arrow; be its mark
Some youthful heart that pines to be beloved."

The jasmine, too, is reputed to be all potent in love matters; and it may be remembered how Moore represents the enchantress Namouna, who was skilled in all manner of charms and talismans, instructing Nourmahal to gather at midnight certain blossoms which would have the effect, when twined into a wreath, of recalling her Selim's love. Accordingly, the flowers having been duly gathered as directed, the enchantress Namouna, whilst singing the following invocatory lines, weaves the mystic chaplet which is to have such wondrous influence:—

"The image of love, that nightly flies
To visit the bashful maid,
Steals from the jasmine flower, that sighs
Its soul, like hers, in the shade.
The dream of a future, or happier, hour
That alights on misery's brow,
Springs out of the almond silvery flower,
That blooms on a leafless bough."

Beans, again, are said to have been accounted efficacious by women as love-producers. An amusing case is recorded of an old woman who was scourged through the streets of Cremona for having endeavoured to conciliate the affections of a young man through the medium of some beans over which mass had been said. In short, all kinds of ingredients appear to have been used in the preparation of these amatory spells, and it is recorded how a young woman, in the seventeenth century, was indicted by the legal authorities of Leipsic for administering a love-philtre composed of bread, hair, and nails to a man whom it seriously affected.

Occasionally confidence was reposed in the power of written charms which were administered in drink, or food, to the person whose love it was desired to secure. Thus the story is told how a young man, passionately enamoured of a damsel of Gaza, having failed in the usual amatory charms, repaired to the priests of Æsculapius, at Memphis, from whom he acquired mystic powers. On returning after a year's absence, he introduced certain magical words and figures cut on Cyprian brass beneath the lady's door. The contrivance had the desired effect, for soon she began to rave on his name, "to wander with uncovered head, and dishevelled hair, for she had become distracted through the vehemence of love."

But cases of this kind were not always attended with the same success. We are told, for instance, how a Norwegian peasant, whose suit had been rejected, sought to inspire the lady he loved with corresponding affection by mystical means. So he carved Runic characters on pieces of wood; but not being sufficiently skilful in this mode of talismanic science, instead of furthering his purpose he threw the damsel into a dangerous illness. Fortunately, a Northern Chief witnessing his sufferings, and, hearing that Runic characters had been carved, sculptured those that he considered more appropriate, which, being placed beneath her pillow, soon restored her again to convalescence.

It is clear that there have been no lack of expedients either for inspiring or dispelling love, many an amusing instance being given in our old romances and folk-tales. It is a Basque superstition that yellow hair in a man is irresistible with a woman; hence every woman who set eyes on Ezkabi Fidel, the golden-haired, fell in love with him. We may compare a curious Irish piece of folk-lore which has long been practised. If a lover will run a hair of the object he loved through the fleshy part of a dead man's leg, the person from whom the hair is taken will go mad with love.

Such a practice may seem ludicrous, but it cannot be forgotten how great a hold it has on the female mind. How far this was originally due to the stories circulated is a matter of uncertainty; but it is generally admitted that tales dealing with the mystic powers of love, and handed down with every semblance of truth, have, in times past, largely helped to propagate a piece of folly which has been productive of so many mischievous effects.

CHAPTER XI

WOMAN'S SECRETS

"Search not to find what lies too deeply hid,
Nor to know things whose knowledge is forbid."
DENHAM.

"TO a woman and a magpie tell what you would speak in the market-place," runs the Spanish proverb—the reason being that "a woman only keeps secret what she does not know;" and therefore an old Latin maxim solemnly enjoins us "not to trust a woman even when dead." Thus Hotspur tells his wife in "I. Henry IV." (act ii. sc. 3):—

"Constant you are,
But yet a woman, and for secrecy
No lady closer; for I well believe
Thou wilt not utter what thou dost not know,
And so far I will trust thee, gentle Kate;"

which, in other words, is equivalent to the well-known German adage, "A woman can't keep a secret, nor let any one else do it." But this maxim cannot be applied only to women, for, as it has been often remarked of secrets, both political and social, they are only too frequently made to be revealed, a truth illustrated by Ben Jonson's words in "The Case is Unaltered," wherein we find this passage:—

> "A secret in his mouth
> Is like a wild bird put into a cage,
> Whose door no sooner opens but 'tis out."

But, whatever dependence is to be placed on a woman's reliability to keep to herself what is told in confidence, it has often been remarked that she can at least keep her own secret, a proof of which will be quickly found if any one question her on the subject of her age.

Apart from this exception, a secret in the keeping of a woman soon becomes what the Spanish are accustomed to call, "The Secret of Anchuelos," that is, one which is known to every one. The town of that name is situated in a gorge between two steep hills, on one of which a shepherd tended his flock, on the other a shepherdess. This pair kept up an amorous converse by bawling from hill to hill, but always with many mutual strict injunctions of secrecy.

The inability of a woman to keep silent what is told her in confidence—even where her husband may be concerned—is exemplified in the once popular saying, "He that tells his wife news is but lately married"—her indiscretion in disclosing information entrusted to her only too frequently causing serious mischief; with which may be compared the Tamil proverb, "Do not disclose your secret to your wife, nor trust your enemy at any time."

But "A wise woman hath a close mouth," which has its equivalent in the French saying, "Le plus sage se tait." According to another popular adage, "Discreet women have neither eyes nor ears," which also has its French parallel, "La femme de bien n'a ny yeux ny orelles."

A piece of proverbial lore which applies to each sex is this: "Tell your secret to your servant and you make him your master"—a maxim which may be traced to an early period when, says Kelly, "it was the policy of the Greek adventurers in Rome to worm out the secrets of the house, and so make themselves feared." Juvenal has referred to this practice:—

> "Poor simple Corydon! do you suppose
> Aught is kept secret that a rich man does?
> If servants hold their tongues, the beasts will blab,
> The dog, the door-posts, and the marble-slab."

Similarly, we find the same proverb on the Continent, "To whom you tell your secret you surrender your freedom;" or, according to another version, "Tell your friend your secret, and he will set his foot on your throat." And it may be remembered Dryden has introduced the same idea:—

> "He who trusts a secret to his servant,
> Makes his own man his master."

African folk-lore, too, introduces the same idea, and a popular proverb says, "If a man tells his secrets to his wife, she will bring him into the way of Satan," which, it has been remarked, is rather a strong contrast to the English proverb, "He who would thrive must ask his wife." And again, it is said, "Trust your dog to the end, a woman till the first opportunity."

As might be supposed, folk-lore, at one time or another, has made good use of the value attaching to secrets; and stories of the supernatural in romantic fiction have shown how the fair sex, under the influence of magical influences, have unknowingly revealed the most sacred secrets. But the moral of most of these tales is the same —and may be applied to either sex—the lesson conveyed being not to trust any one; for, as the French say, "the disclosure of a secret is the fault of him who first disclosed it"—a truth, indeed, which is only too constantly verified in daily life by mistaken trust in another.

Women, it is said, forget the important fact that as soon as a secret becomes the property of three persons it is all the world's, which is summed up in a common Spanish adage, "What three knows every creature knows;" whereas according to the French proverb, "The secret of two is God's secret." The same idea also exists in West Africa, where this proverb is current: "Trust not a woman; she will tell thee what she has just told her companion," and "Whatever be thy intimacy, never give thy heart to a woman."

Turning to some of the numerous folk-tales and legendary stories, in which "the secret" plays the important part, there is the famous one of Melusine, which has been told in many ways. Raymond, Count of Lusignan, was one day hunting the boar in the forest of Poitou, when, whilst wandering in the forest at nightfall through his boar having outstripped his train, he saw Melusine with her sisters, dancing by a fountain in the moonlight. Smitten with her beauty, he asked her to marry him, to which proposal she consented on condition that he would allow her to remain secret and unseen every Sunday. They were married, and her secret was kept until one of his friends suggested that she only desired privacy in order to indulge an adulterous passage. Raymond thereupon burst into her secret chamber and discovered that she was doomed to have the lower part of her body transformed to that of a serpent every Saturday. The secret broken, she was compelled, henceforth, to leave her husband for ever, and to be totally transformed to a serpent. But her spirit continued to haunt the Castle of Lusignan before the death of any of the lords of that race.

Sometimes, on the other hand, the wife is the transgressor. In a North German story a wizard keeps a young girl by force as his wife. One day, accidentally, he lets out the secret that his soul resides in a bird, which is locked up in a church in a desert place, and that, until the bird is killed, he cannot die. The bird is killed by the girl's lover, and the wizard dies—a similar story being found in the "Arabian Nights."

CHAPTER XII

RED-HAIRED GIRLS

"The gold and topaz of the sun on snow
Are shade by the bright hair above those eyes."
PETRARCH.

WHY red hair has been at a discount in all ages has perplexed many a chronicler of fashion. Although, it is true, artists have more chivalrously depicted its beauty, the reverse is the case in literature. What poet, it may be asked, has ventured to sing of "the fair one with the ruddy ringlets" in the same way as the charms of the dark-haired maiden have been so often described?

Whereas the jetty ringlet or flaxen plait has won a thousand admirers, the red-haired girl has found herself persistently passed by. However good and attractive her features, and however graceful her gait may be, she has rarely found her praises acknowledged. Fashion, hitherto, has boycotted in a most unrelenting manner the girl with hair of reddish hue; and, despite the fact that in years gone by many beautiful women possessed tresses of this unaristocratic colour, it still remains unpopular.

It is useless to urge in its favour that Queen Elizabeth considered herself to make the best appearance when wearing a red wig, and that others, counting themselves stars of fashion, have been of the same opinion; for there is a deep-rooted and unaccountable prejudice against this much-abused shade of colour, which it is quite possible some unexpected freak of fashion may one day change. Indeed, from time immemorial, the girl so endowed by Nature has been, in most places, open to sarcasm, and rude unsympathetic passers-by have contemptuously spoken of "carrots" by way of a joke. An old epigram running thus:—

> "Why scorn red hair? The Greeks, we know
> (I note it here in Charity),
> Had taste in beauty, and with them
> The Graces were all 'Charitai.'"

For years past barbers have advertised various compositions for altering the red shade of the hair, and some time ago a high German doctor and astrologer informed the public that he was blessed with a wife "who could make red hair as white as a lily."

A lady whose lover had an unconquerable antipathy to red hair once applied to a noted quack for help in her emergency, who politely answered:—"This is no business of mine, but my wife's, who'll soon redress your grievances and furnish you with a leaden comb, and my anti-Erythræan unguent, which after two or three applications will make you as fair, or as brown, as you please." According to an American newspaper paragraph, twenty-one men in Cincinnati, who had married red-haired women, were found to be colour blind, thus mistaking red for black.

But, going back to the antecedent history of this strange prejudice, it may be traced to a very early period. The Ancient Egyptians, for instance, seem to have been pre-eminent among all nations for their aversion to red-haired people. According to early authorities they were in the habit of annually performing the ceremony of burning alive an unfortunate individual whose only crime was the colour of his hair. "Fancy," as it has been remarked, "the state of mind into which every possessor of the obnoxious shade must have been thrown at the approach of the dreaded ceremony, each not knowing who might be selected as the victim."

From the epithets "red-haired barbarians" and "red-haired devils," with which the Chinese were formerly in the habit of designating the English, it is evident that with them a similar strong antipathy prevailed to this unfortunate, and ill-omened, colour of the hair.

On the other hand, the Romans, from the days of Nero to the present, have been unstinted in their praise of red hair—with the old Romans the colour more esteemed being a dark red, almost brown. Modern Romans, it is said, inherit "the tastes of their ancestors in this respect; and nowhere else on the face of the earth are so many red-haired women to be found as among the patrician families of Rome and Florence. The same liking exists among modern Greeks, who strive to accentuate the burnished effect of their reddish tresses by the wearing of dull gold ornaments."

The Laura whom Petrarch has immortalised attracted him by the colour of her tresses. He first saw her in church clad in a mantle of green, over which her golden red hair fell, which inspired him to write these lines:—

> "The snare was set amidst those threads of gold
> To which Love bound me fast,"

and in another of his songs he says of his lady-love's hair—

> "The gold and topaz of the sun on snow
> Are shade by the bright hair above those eyes."

Spanish artists look with no favour on a red-haired woman, and for two reasons. First, because red hair is in direct opposition to that of the Castilian women, who form the class ideal of feminine beauty to the people of that country. The second reason may be attributed to the old tradition which has led them always to portray Judas as a man with red hair. The same prejudice prevails in France, and Thiers, in his "Histoire des Perruques," gives this as one of the reasons for wearing a wig:—"Les *rousseaux* porterent des perruques pour cacher la couleur de leur cheveux, qui sont en horreur à tout le monde, parceque Judas, à ce qu'on prétend étoit rousseau." Hence there is an old French adage to this effect :—

> "Homme roux et femme barbe,
> Da trente pas loin le salue,
> Avecques trois pierres au poing,
> Pour t'en aider à ton besoign."

In our own country, the literature of past years contains many similar allusions. In "As You Like It," Rosalind, speaking of Orlando, says: "His very hair is of the dissembling colour;" whereupon Celia replies, "Something browner than Judas's." Southey, in his "Vision of the Maid of Orleans," after having taken the poor girl to a number of unpleasant places, introduces her to the following disagreeable personage :—

> "From thence they came
> Where, in the next ward, a most wretched band
> Groaned underneath the bitter tyranny
> Of a fierce demon. His coarse hair was red,
> Pale grey his eyes, and bloodshot, and his face
> Wrinkled with such a smile as malice wears
> In ecstasy."

This demon, of course, is Cruelty, into whose charge are committed all those who have been guilty of cruelty in their lifetime. Shirley, in his "Doubtful Heir," expresses the same idea, as also does Dryden, in his play of "Amboyna." Middleton, too, in his "Chaste Maid of Cheapside," has a similar allusion, showing how popular and widespread was the prejudice to this unfortunate colour; indeed, so much so, that there is some reason to think that the devil himself had occasionally this attribute bestowed upon him.

The Brahmins were forbidden to marry a red-haired woman; and, as it has been remarked, "the populace of most countries, confounding moral with æsthetic impressions, accuses red-haired people of various shortcomings." Hence, superstition has assigned to hair of a coppery tinge, when it adorns a woman's head, the worst traits; and "all the petty vices, all the lamentable shortcomings to which femininity is heir have been laid to the charge of the reddish crown." Of course this is only prejudice; and as the author of the "Ugly Girl Papers" writes, "I have seen a most obnoxious head of colour so changed by a few years' care that it became the admiration of the owner's friends, and could hardly be recognised as the withered, fiery locks once worn." At the same time there seems some truth in the common opinion that a red-haired girl is invariably self-conscious; for she knows that her hair, although it may not be of a fiery carrot colour, is the subject of daily comment.

Referring to the colour of the hair in folk-lore, we may note that from time immemorial there has been a strong antipathy to red hair, which, according to some antiquarians, originated in a tradition that Judas had hair of this colour. One reason, it has been suggested, why the dislike to it arose was that it was considered ugly and unfashionable, and on this account a person with red hair would soon be regarded with contempt. It has been conjectured, too, that the odium took its rise from the aversion to the red-haired Danes.

Yellow hair was, also, in years gone by, regarded with ill-favour, and almost esteemed a deformity, allusions to which prejudice are of constant occurrence ; and, it may be added, that hair was often used metaphorically for the colour, complexion, or nature of a thing, as in Beaumont and Fletcher's "The Nice Valour"—

"A lady of my hair cannot want pitying."

CHAPTER XIII

WOMAN'S FICKLENESS

"Ladies, like variegated tulips, show
'Tis to their changes half their charms we owe."
POPE'S *Moral Essays*, Ep. ii.

BY an unwritten law it is held to be the privilege of woman to change her mind, a licence of which she rarely fails to avail herself. Hence she has often been said to be chameleon-like, and, as a German proverb runs, "Women are variable as April weather;" a Sindhi proverb used of fickle-minded people being this: "A mad woman wears a bangle sometimes on the arm and sometimes on the leg;" of which there are other versions, as thus:—

"Maids are May when they are maids,
But the sky changes when they are wives."

and, "Fortune is like woman, loves youth, and is fickle."

According to an old adage in this country, "A

woman's mind and winter wind change oft;" or, as it is sometimes said, "Winter weather and woman's thoughts often change;" another version of which we find current in Spain, "Women, wind, and fortune soon change;" and, similarly, it is said, "She can laugh and cry both in a wind."

But it has apparently always been so, and Virgil describes woman as "ever variable, ever changeable," and likens her to Proteus—

> "Caeneus, a woman once, and once a man,
> But ending in the sex she first began."

Similarly, Verdi, in his opera of "Rigoletto," speaks of woman as an inconstant thing. Catullus, again, was of opinion that, "What a woman says to her ardent lover ought to be written on the winds, or on running water," so shifting and transient are her vows and professions, which reminds us of Keats's epitaph—

> "Here lies one whose name was writ in water."

This failing has been made the subject of frequent comment and ridicule, and Pope tells us how—

> "Papillia, wedded to her amorous spark,
> Sighs for the shadow—'How charming is a park!'
> A park is purchas'd, but the fair he sees
> All bath'd in tears—'O odious, odious trees.'"

The French popular adage says, "Woman often varies, fool is he who trusts her." The story goes that these words were written by Francis I. on a window-pane in the Castle of Chambord. His sister, Queen Margaret of Navarre, entered as he was writing what she considered a slander on her sex, and declared that she could quote twenty instances of man's infidelity. But Francis replied that her words were not to the point, and that he would rather hear one instance of a woman's constancy; to which the Queen replied, "Can you mention a single instance of her inconstancy?"

Francis triumphantly answered in the affirmative, for it so happened that, a few weeks before this conversation, a gentleman of the Court had been thrown into prison on a serious charge, while his wife, who was one of the Queen's ladies-in-waiting, was reported to have eloped with his page.

Margaret, however, maintained that the lady was innocent, at which the King shook his head, at the same time promising that if, within a month, her character should be re-established, he would break the pane on which the disputed words were written, and grant his sister any favour she might ask. Not many days had elapsed when it was discovered that it was not the lady who had fled with the page, but her husband. During one of her visits to him in prison they had exchanged clothes, whereby he was enabled to deceive the jailer and effect his escape, while his devoted wife remained in his place.

Margaret claimed his pardon at the King's hand, who not only granted it, but gave a grand fête and tournament to celebrate this instance of conjugal affection. He also destroyed the pane of glass, although the saying on it has long passed into a proverb. It may, however, be added that Brantôme, who had seen the writing, says that the words were "Toute femme varie," and not a distich, as is commonly supposed :—

"Souvent femme varie,
Bien fou qui s'y fie."

On the other hand, Sir Philip Sidney was one of those who was forced to admit woman's fickleness, for he thus writes :—

"He water ploughs, and soweth in the sand,
And hopes the flickering wind with net to hold,
Who hath his hopes laid on a woman's hand."

Again, the unreliability of woman has been exemplified in the saying, "An eel's held by the tail surer than a woman ;" a maxim which is said to be "an ancient truth" in Field's "Amends for Ladies," published in the year 1618, and is much to the same effect as the following lines :—

"She will and she will not. She grants, denies,
Consents, retracts, advances, and then flies."

And an Oriental proverb says that "Women are like bows, they can bend as much as they please ;" in other words, they are as changeable as the moon. But, although the proverbial lore of most countries makes fickleness one of the grave defects of a woman's character, it may be questioned whether, in this respect, she is a more grievous offender than man, despite all that has been said to prove her the greater sinner. However much, too, poets after the manner of Charles Mackay may have spoken of woman's fickleness in words like the following :—

"Whene'er a woman vows to love you
In fortune's spite ;
Make protestations that would prove you
Her soul's delight ;
Swears that no other love shall win her
By passion stirr'd ;
Believe her not ;—the charming sinner
Will break her word ;"

it must not be forgotten that the same charge has been made against man, and oftentimes in language still more severe, an illustration of which may be quoted from Dryden's "Absalom and Ahitophel" :—

"A man so various, that he seem'd to be
Not one, but all mankind's epitome ;
Stiff in opinions, always in the wrong ;
Was everything by starts, and nothing long ;
But, in the course of one revolving moon,
Was chemist, fiddler, statesman, and buffoon ;
Then all for women, painting, rhyming, drinking,
Besides ten thousand freaks that died in thinking."

And yet the fair sex has always been credited with being fickle, one popular cure for which, in olden times, was the love-philtre, or potion, which forms the subject of a preceding chapter.

CHAPTER XIV

LOCAL ALLUSIONS TO WOMEN

" He that will not merry be,
With a pretty girl by the fire,
I wish he was atop of Dartemoor
A-stugged in the mire."
Devonshire Folk-Rhyme.

MANY of our old towns and villages throughout the country have long been famous for certain characteristics, and some of these which pay special honour to the fair sex are embodied in local rhymes, which, if not in all respects quite complimentary, are generally quaint and good-humoured.

A popular folk-rhyme informs us :—

" Oxford for learning, London for a wit,
Hull for women, and York for a tit."

The downs in the vicinity of Sutton, Banstead, and Epsom, in addition to being noted for their small sheep, which have given rise to various rhymes, have been in other ways equally famous, if we are to believe the following :—

"Sutton for good mutton,
Cheam for juicy beef,
Croydon for a pretty girl,
And Mitcham for a thief."

But these are not the only places, as other folk-rhymes tell us, that can lay claim to producing pretty girls ; for, under Oxfordshire, in Halliwell's "Nursery Rhymes of England," these lines are given :—

"King's Sutton is a pretty town,
And lies all in a valley ;
It has a pretty ring of bells,
Besides a bowling alley ;
Wine in liquor in good store,
Pretty maidens plenty,
Can a man desire more ?
There ain't such a town in twenty ;"

with which may be compared a similar rhyme on Middlewych, in Cheshire :—

"Middlewych is a pretty town,
Seated in a valley,
With a church and market cross,
And eke a bowling alley.
All the men are loyal there,
Pretty girls are plenty,
Church and King, and down with the Rump—
There's not such a town in twenty."

Chambers, in his "Popular Rhymes of Scotland,"

quotes an old rhyme descriptive of places in the parishes of Bunkle and Chirnside; "but, alas," he says, "five of these little farm towns no longer exist, their lands being now included in large possessions:—

> "Little Billy, Billy Mill,
> Billy Mains, and Billy Hill,
> Ashfield and Auchencraw,
> Bullerhead and Pefferlaw,
> There's bonny lasses in them a'."

The term, "Lancashire fair women," has long ago become proverbial, in connection with which we may quote this note by Ray: "Whether the women of this county be indeed fairer than their neighbours I know not, but that the inhabitants of some counties may be, and are, generally fairer than those of others, is most certain; the reason whereof is to be attributed partly to the temperature of the air, partly to the condition of the soil, and partly to their manner of food. The hotter the climate, generally the blacker the inhabitants, and the colder, the fairer; the colder, I say, to a certain degree, for in extreme cold countries the inhabitants are of dusky complexions. But in the same climate, that in some places the inhabitants should be fairer than in others, proceeds from the diversity of the situation—either high or low, maritime or far from sea—or of the soil and manner of living, which we see have so much influence upon hearts, as to alter in them bigness, shape, and colour; and why it may not have the like on men I see not."

Another folk-rhyme tells us :—

> "Barton under Needwood,
> Dunstall in the Dale;
> Sitenhill for a pretty girl,
> And Burton for good ale;"

which is similar to one told of the hamlets of Pulverbatch, in Shropshire :—

> "Cothercot up o' the hill,
> Wilderley down i' the dale,
> Churton for pretty girls,
> And Powtherbitch for good ale."

"Suffolk fair maids" is another popular proverbial expression, an allusion to which we find in Greene's "Friar Bacon and Friar Bungay" (Works, Edit. 1861, p. 153):—

> "A bonnier wench all Suffolk cannot yield.
> All Suffolk! Nay, all England holds none such;"

and Ray remarks on this expression: "It seems the God of Nature hath been bountiful in giving them beautiful complexions; which I am willing to believe, so far forth as it fixeth not a comparative disparagement on the same sex in other places."

On the other hand, we occasionally find a place mentioned as possessing no pretty girls, as in the following :—

> "Halifax is made of wax,
> And Heptonstall of stone;
> In Halifax there's many a pretty girl
> In Heptonstall there's none."

A humorous rhyme on Camberwell runs thus :—

"All the maides in Camberwell,
May daunce in an egge shell,
For there are no maydes in that well ;"

to which one, who, it has been suggested, was doubtless a Camberwellian, answered in clumsy doggerel :—

"All the maides in Camberwell towne,
Cannot daunce in an acre of ground." [1]

It is proverbially said, too :—

"Castleford women must needs be fair,
Because they wash both in Calder and Aire."

In short, in accordance with an old adage, "England's the Paradise of Women," upon which Ray has this note : "And well it may be called so, as might easily be demonstrated in many particulars, were not all the world therein satisfied. Hence it has been said that if a bridge were made over the narrow seas, all the women in Europe would come over hither. Yet it is worth the noting, that though in no country in the world the men are so fond of, so much governed by, so wedded to their wives, yet hath no language so many proverbial invectives against women."

Some places have enjoyed the unenviable notoriety

[1] Northall's "English Folk-Rhymes," p. 45.

of possessing loose women, if we are to put reliance in folk-rhymes like the subjoined :—

"Beccles for a puritan, Bungay for the poor,
Halesworth for a drunkard, and Bilborough for a whore."

According to a Leicestershire saying, "There are more whores in Hose, than honest women in Long Clawton ;" the humour of this proverb, as Ray says, 'turning on the word hose, which is here meant to signify stockings, and is the name of a small village adjoining Long Clawton, which is comparatively very populous." A proverbial couplet current in Essex informs us :—

"Braintree for the pure, and Bocking for the poor ;
Cogshall for the jeering town, and Kelvedon for the whore."

And to give a further instance, a Surrey folk-rhyme is to this effect :—

"Sutton for mutton, Carshalton for beeves,
Epsom for whores, and Ewel for thieves."

At one time, too, it was a common saying, "Who goes to Westminster for a wife, to Paul's for a man, and to Smithfield for a horse, may meet with a whore, a knave, and a jade ;" with which may be compared the following old folk-rhyme on the Inns of Court :—

"The Inner Temple rich,
The Middle Temple poor :
Lincoln's Inn for law,
And Gray's Inn for a whore."

Herefordshire has long been famous for its four W's—its wine (cider), its wood (its sylvan scenery), its women, and its water (the river Wye), whence the saying, "Wine, wood, women, and water;" and a popular couplet speaks of :—

"Oxford knives,
London wives";

which, according to Grose, would seem to imply that "the Oxford knives were better to look at than to cut with; and that the London wives had more beauty and good breeding than housewifely qualities," with which may be compared a similar folk-rhyme :—

"Hutton for auld wives,
Broadmeadows for swine;
Paxton for drunken wives,
And salmon sae fine."

Cheshire people when referring to a girl noted for her good looks are wont to describe her as being "As fair as Lady Done," a phrase which is thus explained by Pennant, in his "Journey from Chester to London," 1793 :—"Sir John Done, Knight, hereditary forester and keeper of the forest of Delamere, Cheshire, died in 1629. When James I. made a progress in the year 1607, he was entertained by this gentleman at Utkinton, etc. He married Dorothy, daughter of Thomas Wilbraham, Esq., of Woodhey, who left behind her so admirable a character, that to this day, when a Cheshire man would express some excellency in one of the fair sex, he would say, 'There is Lady Done for you.'"

Ray, also, tells us that, "The Dones were a great family in Cheshire, living at Utkinton, by the forest side. Nurses use there to call their children so, if girls; if boys, Earls of Derby."

It is also commonly said in Cheshire, "Better wed over the mixen than over the moor"—a proverbial adage which Ray thus explains: "That is, hard by, or at home—the mixon being that heap of compost which lies in the yards of good husbandmen—than far off, or from London. The road from Chester leading to London over some part of the moorlands in Staffordshire, the meaning is, that gentry in Cheshire find it more profitable to match within their own county, than to bring a bride out of other shires: (1) Because better acquainted with her birth and breeding. (2) Because though her portion may chance to be less to maintain her, such inter-marriages in this county have been observed both a prolonger of worshipful families and the preserver of amity between them."

We find the same proverb in Scotland, "Better over the midden than over the muir;" and it has also found its way to the Continent, for to a young person about to marry in Germany this advice is given, "Marry over the mixon, and you will know who and what she is;" with which may be compared the Italian admonition, "Your wife and your nag get from a neighbour."

A couplet popular in Wem, Shropshire, runs thus :—

> "The women of Wem, and a few musketeers,
> Beat Lord Capel, and all his cavaliers."

Wem was the first town in Shropshire to declare for the Parliament. The story told—which gave rise to this rhyme—is that in 1643, Lord Capel, the King's lieutenant-general in Wales and the border counties, attempted to seize it from Shrewsbury before the completion of the fortifications, but he was repulsed from Wem by about forty troopers, with the aid of the townspeople. A smart piece of deception, it is said, was adopted, for old women in red cloaks were posted at carefully-selected spots, thus scaring the enemy, who took them for soldiers.

Another Cheshire adage tells us, "When the daughter is stolen, shut Pepper Gate," which Grose thus explains—"Pepper Gate was a postern on the east side of the city of Chester. The mayor of the city having his daughter stolen away by a young man through that gate, whilst she was playing at ball with the other maidens, his worship, out of revenge, caused it to be closed up."

There are numerous items of folk-lore of a similar character ; and the Scotch, when speaking of a changeable woman, remark, "Ye're as fu' o' maggots as the bride of Preston, wha stopt half-way as she gaed to the kirk ;" on which adage, Henderson writes : "We have not been able to learn who the bride of Preston really was, but we have frequently heard the saying applied to young women who are capricious and changeable :—

> "The bride took a maggot, it was but a maggot,
> She wadna gang by the west mains to be married."

Another common expression is, "Take a seat on Maggy Shaw's Crocky," which is a broad, flat stone, near to the brink of a precipice, overhanging the seashore, about a mile to the north of Eyemouth. Tradition says this stone was placed over the remains of an old woman who had hanged herself, and who is said frequently to be seen at night resting upon it, in the shape of a white sea-mew, sitting lonely on the—

> "Glitty stane,
> Green with the dow o' the jauping main."

Sometimes one may hear a Scotch peasant use the phrase, "Ye breed o' Lady Mary, when you're gude, ye're ower gude," which Kelly thus explains: "A drunken man one day begged Lady Mary to help him on his horse, and having made many attempts to no purpose, he always reiterated the same position; at length he jumped quite over. 'O, Lady Mary,' said he, 'when thou art good, thou art over good.'" Another common phrase is, "Gae kiss your lucky—she lives in Leith," which Allan Ramsay thus explains: "A cant phrase, from what rise I know not, but it is made use of when persons think it is not worth while to give a distinct answer, or think themselves foolishly accused."

It is commonly said in Buckinghamshire, in reference to a marriage of unequal age, "An old man who marries a buxom young maiden bids fair to become a freeman of Buckingham," that is, a cuckold. A Shropshire proverb, in which there does not seem to be much point, says, "He that fetches a wife from Shrewsbury must carry her into Staffordshire, or else he shall live in Cumberland," with which may be compared the following old rhyme :—

"Women are born in Wiltshire,
Brought up in Cumberland,
Lead their lives in Bedfordshire,
Bring their husbands to Buckingham,
And die in Shrewsbury."

On the Kentish coast the white clouds which commonly bring rain are nicknamed "Folke Stone Washerwomen ;" and in Cornwall we find the expression, "Grained like a Wellcombe woman ;"—Wellcombe is about three miles from Morwenstow, the women in this neighbourhood being remarkably dark. At the present day, too, one may often hear the Sussex peasantry use the phrase, "Lithe as a lass of Kent," and in Northamptonshire a current expression used to be, "She is quite an Amy Florence."

Another old proverbial phrase which, at one time or another, has given rise to much discussion is, "As long as Meg of Westminster," which, says Ray, "is applied to persons very tall, especially if they have hopple height wanting breadth proportionately. But that there ever was," he adds, "such a giant woman cannot be proved by any good witness. I pass not for a late lying pamphlet, entitled, 'Story of a monstrous tall Virago called "Long Megg of Westminster,"' the writer of which thinks it might relate to a great gun lying in the Tower, called Long Megg, in troublesome times brought to Westminster, where for some time it continued."

Fuller, writing in 1662, says, "The large gravestone shown on the south side of the cloister in Westminster Abbey, said to cover her body, was placed over a number of monks who died of the plague, and were all buried in one grave."

Turning once more to Scotland, there is a small village named Ecclesmagirdle, situated "under the northern slope of the Ochil Hills, and for some considerable part of the year untouched by the solar rays." Hence the following rhyme :—

"The lasses o' Exmagirdle
May very weel be dun ;
For frae Michaelmas till Whitsunday,
They never see the sun."

Corncairn, situated in Banffshire, is an extensive and fertile district, adjacent to Cornhill, where the well-known Cornhill markets are held. It was long noted for the industry of its inhabitants and the thrift of its women, which seems to have given rise to the following folk-rhyme :—

"A' the wives o' Corncairn,
Drilling up their harn yarn ;
They hae corn, they hae kye,
They have webs o' claith, for bye."

In Gilburn, Linlithgowshire, there is current a curious traditionary couplet. The story goes that an unfortunate lady lived with a Duke of Hamilton, very many years ago, at Kinneil House. She is said to have put an end to her existence by throwing herself from the walls of the castle into the deep ravine below, through which the Gilburn descends. Her spirit is supposed to haunt this glen; and it has long been customary for the children in the neighbourhood, on dark and stormy nights, to say:—

> "Lady, Lady Lilburn,
> Hunts in the Gilburn."

But, it has been suggested, it is far more likely that Lady Lilburn was the wife of the celebrated Cromwellian colonel, who for a time occupied Kinneil House.

Similarly, a dishonest milk-woman at Shrewsbury, who is condemned to wander up and down Lady Studeley's Diche, in the Raven Meadow—now the Smithfield—is said to repeat this couplet:—

> "Weight and measure sold I never,
> Milk and water sold I ever";

which at Burslem, in the Stafford-shire, has been associated with an old witch, locally known as "Old Molly Lee."

CHAPTER XV

WOMAN'S WILL

"He is a fool who thinks by force or skill
To turn the current of a woman's will."
TUKE, *The Adventures of Five Hours.*

IT has been humorously remarked—although it must have been prior to the time when the law invested womankind with testamentary powers—"That women must have their wills while they live, because they make none when they die." Butler, in his "Miscellaneous Thoughts," amusingly remarks :—

"The souls of women are so small
That some believe they've none at all ;
Or, if they have, like cripples still,
They've but one faculty, the will."

It is generally acknowledged that, however many a woman's deficiencies may be, she is not wanting in a will. Indeed, the strength of a woman's will has been admitted even by her opponents; and the French have a saying that, "What a woman wills, God wills;" with which may be compared the familiar Italian adage, "Whatever a woman will she can," reminding us of the rhyme on a pillar at Canterbury :—

"Where is the man who has the power and skill
To stem the torrent of a woman's will?
For if she will, she will, you may depend on't,
And if she won't, she won't, so there's an end on't."

According to another version of the same proverbial rhyme, we are told :—

"The man's a fool who tries by force or skill
To stem the current of a woman's will,
For if she will, she will, you may depend on't,
And if she won't, she won't, and there's an end on't;"

which reminds us of what Terence wrote: "I know what a woman's temper is: When you will, they won't: and when you won't, then they are in a perfect fever the other way."

Hence there is a world-wide saying to the effect that, "Swine, women, and bees are not to be turned." But Schiller, it would seem, was one of those who was bold enough to deny the sovereignty of a woman's will, for he says, "Man is the only being who can will;" whereas, to quote a not very complimentary phrase current in years past, it is said "She-devils are hard to turn." How important it was once considered that a woman's will should be directed aright may be gathered from this adage, "It shall be at the wife's will if the husband thrive," or, according to another version, "He that will thrive must ask leave of his wife," which we find embodied in the following couplet which occurs in "The Tale of the Basyn"[1]—

"Hit is an olde seid saw, I swere be Seynt Tyue,
Hit shall be at the wyve's will if the husbande thryue."

It is further alluded to by Francis Dudley, 4th Lord North, in his "Observations and Advices Œconomical" (1669, p. 4): "It is an ancient English proverb, that if a man will thrive he must ask leave of his wife, and thrift is a matter of no small consideration in œconomy. If, therefore, choice be made of a wife, let him use as well his ear as his eye, that is, let him trust to his discretion, according to what he hears, than to his affection kindled by sight."

And yet a woman does not always know her own mind; for, as it is said, "Maids say nay and take," or, as it has been observed in a previous chapter, "A woman's mind and winter change oft;" an amusing illustration of the indecision of a woman's will being given by Kelly in the following anecdote, which is from a Latin sermon on widowhood by Jean Raulin, a monk of Cluny, of the fifteenth century, a story which has been retold by Rabelais:—

"A widow consulted her parish priest about her entering into a second marriage. She told him she stood in need of a helpmate and protector, and that her journeyman, for whom she had taken a fancy, was industrious and well acquainted with her late husband's trade.

[1] Hazlitt's "Popular Poetry," iii. p. 45.

" 'Very well,' said the priest, 'you had better marry him.'

" 'And yet,' rejoined the widow, 'I am afraid to do it, for who knows but I may find my servant become my master?'

" 'Well then,' said the priest, 'don't have him.'

" 'But what shall I do,' said the widow; 'the business left me by my poor, dear, departed husband is more than I can manage by myself.'

" 'Marry him, then,' said the priest.

" 'Ay, but suppose he turns out a scamp,' said the widow; 'he may get hold of my property and run through it all.'

" 'Don't have him,' said the priest.

"Thus the dialogue went on, the priest always agreeing in the last opinion expressed by the widow, until at length, seeing that her mind was actually made up to marry the journeyman, he told her to consult the church bells, and they would advise her best what to do.

"Accordingly the bells were rung, and the widow heard them distinctly say, 'Do take your man; do take your man.'

"She went home and married him forthwith; but it was not long before he thrashed her soundly, and made her feel that instead of his mistress she had become his servant.

"Back she went to the priest, cursing the hour when she had been credulous enough to act upon his advice.

" 'Good woman,' said he, 'I am afraid you did not rightly understand what the bells said to you.'

He rang them again, and then the poor woman heard clearly, but too late, these warning words: 'Do not take him; do not take him.'"

Vacillating, at times, as a woman's will may be, it is proverbially difficult to turn, especially when bent on some special object. Hence Edmund Spenser says:—

"Extremely mad the man, I surely deem,
That weens with watch and hard restraint to stay
A woman's will, which is disposed to go astray."

Two women, it is said, never think alike; and, as each wishes to have a will of her own, we can understand the truth of the following folk-rhyme, to which reference has been made elsewhere:—

"Two women in one house,
Two cats and one mouse,
Two dogs and one bone,
Will never accord in one"—

a piece of proverbial wisdom of which there are several versions, one of which occurs in the "Book of St. Albans," 1486 (reprinted 1881), and, "Although most women," as the adage says, "be long-lived, yet they all die with an ill-will." At any rate, if there be truth in the Scotch proverb, it seems a woman must have her way occasionally, for, "Gie her her will, or she'll burst," quoth the man when his wife knocked his head with the three-legged stool.

Indeed, it has been generally acknowledged that the most difficult thing to manage is a woman's will, for, according to a Hindustani proverb, "The obstinacy of a woman, a child, and a king is not to be overcome;" with which may be compared the Kashmiri proverb which tells us that, "A contrary woman is like bad grass on the roof," the meaning being that grass which is not adapted for thatching does not set well. And we may compare an old English couplet:—

"To talk well with some women doth as much good
As a sick man to eat up a load of green wood."

Which, says Mr. Halliwell,[1] is the same class of dictum as that which occurs in the "Schole-house of Women," 1541:—

"As holsome for a man is a woman's corse
As a shoulder of mutton for a sick horse."

And once more, according to the Lancashire adage, a woman's will is thus summed up:—

"Many men has many minds,
But women has but two;
Everything is what they'd have,
And nothing would they do."

[1] "English Proverbs," p. 433.

CHAPTER XVI

WOMEN AND MARRIAGE

"Be sure before you marry
Of a house wherein to tarry."
Old Proverb.

SIR JOHN MORE, the famous Chancellor's father, once wrote: "I would compare the multitude of women which are to be chosen for wives unto a bag full of snakes, having among them a single eel: now, if a man should put his hand into this bag, he may chance to light on the eel, but it is an hundred to one he shall be stung by the snake"—a statement which finds its exact parallel in the proverb, "Put your hand in the creel, and take out either an adder or an eel," an idea as old as the time of Juvenal—

"What! Posthumus take a wife? What fury drest
With snakes for hair has your poor brain possest?"

Severe as this statement may seem, it must be remembered that it was a woman—Lady Wortley

Montagu—thus gave expression to much the same sentiment: "It goes far towards reconciling me to being a woman, when I reflect that I am thus in no immediate danger of ever marrying one."

"With most marriages," remarked Goëthe, "it is not long till things assume a very piteous look," which is to the same effect as the French adage: "Wedlock rides in the saddle, and repentance on the croup;" with which may be compared our own proverb, "Maids want nothing but husbands, and, when they have them, they want everything."

Selden looked upon marriage as "a desperate thing;" and he tells us that "the frogs in Æsop were extremely wise, they had a great mind to some water, but they would not leap into the well, because they could not get out again;" and a humorous description of marriage, much to the same point, has been left us by Sir John Davies in the "Contention":—

"Wedlock hath oft compared been
  To public feasts, where meet a public rout,
Where they that are without would fain go in,
  And they that are within would fain go out.

Or to the jewel which this virtue had,
  That men were mad till they might it obtain,
But, when they had it, they were twice as mad,
  Till they were dispossessed of it again."

The Scotch say, "Married folks are like rats in a trap, fain to get ithers in, but fain to be out themsels," an allusion to which we find in the "Tea Table Miscellany":—

> "Of all comforts I miscarried,
> When I played the sot and married;
> 'Tis a trap, there's none need doubt on't,
> Those that are in would fain get out on't."

And from the earliest period the same unfavourable view has been taken of marriage, Juvenal apeaking of it as the "matrimonial halter." It was popularly said that "marriage is an evil that men pray for," and, according to another common adage, "Marriage, if one consider the truth, is an evil, but a necessary evil;" an amusing illustration of the prudent man being found in one of Martial's epigrams:—

> "You'd marry the marquis, fair lady, they say;
> You are right; we've suspected it long:
> But his lordship declines in a complaisant way,
> And, faith, he's not much in the wrong."

Heyne quaintly wrote: "The music at a marriage procession always reminds me of the music which leads soldiers to battle," which is borne out by the adage: "The married man must turn his staff into a stake." Lord Burleigh's advice to his son, too, was similar: "In choosing thy wife, use great prudence and circumspection, for from thence will spring all thy future good or evil;" and it is "an action of life like unto a stratagem of war, wherein a man can *err* but once"—a timely warning we find embodied in the old proverb:—

> "Who weddeth ere he be wise,
> Shall die ere he thrive;"

and in the adage, "Choose a wife rather by your ear than your eye."

Then there is the Spanish woman's opinion of marriage, who, when asked by her daughter, "What sort of a thing is marriage?" replied: "Daughter, it is spinning, bearing children, and weeping;" which is only another mode of expression for the subjoined folk-rhyme :—

> "When a couple are newly married,
> The first month is honeymoon, or smick-smack.
> The second is hither and thither, the third is thwick-thwack.
> The fourth, the devil take them that brought thee and I together."

There are numerous rhymes of this sort which do not reflect favourably on the fair sex. A couplet still often quoted to young people anxious for matrimony tells them :—

> "Needles and pins, needles and pins,
> When a man marries his trouble begins;"

with which may be compared the Syrian maxim, "Girl, do not exult in thy wedding dress; see how much trouble lurks behind it." Indeed, of the host of sayings respecting marriage contained in the proverbial lore of our own and other countries, the greater part take a very pessimistic view of married life—"Age and wedlock tame man and beast," and "Age and wedlock we all desire and repent of" However much the conjugal lot may be envied, the consensus of opinion appears to be that "Age and wedlock bring a man to his nightcap." Hence it is said, "He who marrieth doth well, but he who marrieth not, better."

On the Continent it is said, "Grief for a dead wife lasts to the doors," and according to a popular rhyme—

"Two good days for a man in this life—
When he weds and when he buries his wife."

The French adage runs: "He that hath a wife hath strife;" and the Spanish people say that "A man's best fortune, or his worst, is his wife." There is a well-known couplet which tells us—

"He who repents him not of his marriage, sleeping or wakin', in a year and a day,
May lawfully go to Dunmow, and fetch a gammon of bacon;"

in allusion to the custom of applying for the "Dunmow Flitch," a curious account of which—from a MS. in the College of Arms—will be found in the "Antiquarian Repertory" (1807, iii. p. 342). Hence originated the proverbial rhyme—

"Who fetcheth a wife from Dunmow
Carrieth home two sides of a sow."

Indeed, one French proverb has gone so far as to affirm that "Marriage is the sunset of love," one reason for this failure being the many impediments, it is argued, which in most cases, under one form or another, are certain sooner or later to militate against the harmony of the marriage state. An obstacle, for instance, to married happiness is the mother-in-law, for as the oft-quoted rhyme says :—

> "Of all the old women that ever I saw,
> Sweet bad luck to my mother-in-law."

The New Forest folks say, "There is but one good mother-in-law, and she is dead;" which is the same as the German proverb, "There is no good mother-in-law but she that wears a green gown," *i.e.*, covered with the grass of the churchyard ; or, as another version has it, "The best mother-in-law is she on whose gown the geese feed."

Among further illustrations of the same old belief, it is said that "Mother-in-law and daughter-in-law are a tempest and hailstorm ;" and the Dutch say, "The husband's mother is the wife's devil." Accordingly, the Spanish say of a girl who has no relatives by marriage, "She is well married who has neither mother-in-law nor sister-in-law by a husband." This, indeed, would seem to be the testimony of all ages and countries, which, as it has been pointed out, is all the more remarkable, because "the mother-in-law remembers not that she was once herself a daughter-in-law."

Marriage not infrequently brings want, for we are told that even "A wee house has a wide throat," and "A poor wedding is a prologue to misery." "It is easier to build two chimneys than to maintain one"—that is, it is easier to build two chimneys than keep one wife runs another old saw, and the Portuguese say, "Marry, marry, and what about the housekeeping?" for, as our proverb says:—

> "Want makes strife
> 'Twixt man and wife,"

which is another form of the well-known couplet:—

> "Nothing agreeth worse
> Than a lady's heart and a beggar's purse;"

since, as the proverb goes, "Haste makes waste, and waste makes want, and want makes strife between the goodman and his wife." But there is some consolation in the fact handed down by the wise men of old, "He's that needy when he is married, shall be rich when he is buried." Despite, however, what proverbial literature may have to say respecting marriage, we must not forget the old belief that "Marriage is destiny," a piece of fatalism to which, it may be remembered, Shakespeare alludes:—

> "The ancient saying is no heresy,
> Hanging and wiving go by destiny."

This notion is very old, and in the "Schole-hous of Women," published in 1541, we find it thus noticed:—

> "Truely some men there be
> That live always in some great honour,
> And say, it goeth by destiny,
> To hang or wed: both hath but one hour."

Heywood, in his "If you Know not Me," etc.

(1605), says: "Everyone to his fortune as men go to hanging." It is, too, the same as the Scottish adage, "Hanging gangs by hap;" but, as Hazlitt remarks, "that polite nation has agreed to omit the other portion, perhaps as implying an incivility to the fair sex."

Another form of the same piece of folk-lore is the popular English saying, "Marriages are made in heaven;" or, as the French version has it, "Marriages are written in heaven;" the meaning being, as Kelly says, "that it is not forethought, inclination, or mutual fitness that has the largest share in bringing man and wife together; more efficient than all these is the force of circumstances, or what people vaguely call chance, fate, fortune, and so forth." We find the same belief prevalent in Italy, and it is equivalent to the Scotch adage: "A man may woo where he will, but must wed where he's weird"—that is, where he is fated to wed. The Irish also have a proverb that "Marriage comes unawares, like a soot-drop;" wherein, as it has been pointed out by a correspondent of *Notes and Queries*, there is "an allusion to the rain finding its way through the thatch, blackened by the smoke of the peat fires;" a similar version of which we find elsewhere:—

"In time she comes whom God sends."

If it be true that marriages are made in heaven, an old humorous proverb adds this rider: "If marriages are made in heaven, you have but few friends there."

Since marriage, however, as already stated, is an indispensable necessity, proverb-philosophers have framed a host of curious maxims for the guidance of those desirous of taking what they hold to be the fatal step. Thus a young lady is reminded that she had—

> "Better be an old man's darling
> Than a young man's warling;"

or, as modern collections of proverbs read, for "warling," "snarling;" another version running thus: "Better have an old man to humour than a young man to break your heart." And, alluding to young wives, we may quote a Dutch proverb—

> "Two cocks in one house, two cats and a mouse,
> And an old man and a young wife are always in strife;"

a version of which we find among the Hindu proverbs—

> "Two cats and one mouse, and rival wives in a house,
> And two dogs with one bone, can never get on together;"

to which must be added the solemn German warning: "A young wife is an old man's post-horse to the grave;" or, as another version puts it: "An old man who marries a young woman gives an invitation to death."

Indeed, the proverbial lore of most countries is to the same effect, the well-known adage reminding us that "crabbed age and youth cannot live together." Even the Sindhi maxim is similar:

"No use marrying an old man and wasting life, for while wheat crops are being reaped he would break down;" with which we may compare the familiar maxims, "Grey and green make the worst medley," and "An old man who weds a buxom young maiden bids fair to become a freeman of Buckingham"—that is, a cuckold.

There is something like it in Scotland, where it is said, "His auld brass will buy her a new pan," spoken of young girls who marry wealthy old men, meaning that when the husband dies his money will help her to a younger one, an allusion to which occurs in the "Tea Table Miscellany"—

> "Though auld Rob Morris be an elderly man,
> Yet his auld brass it will buy you a new pan;
> Then, daughter, you shouldna be so ill to shoo,
> For auld Rob Morris is the man you maun loo."

The selection of one of the fair sex for the married state has been made the subject of special warning, and we are told that "He has great need of a wife that marries mamma's darling," and "He that goes a great way for a wife is either cheated, or means to cheat."

Conventional marriages have found no favour in proverbial wisdom, for, as the old adage runs—

> "Wedlock without love, they say,
> Is but a lock without a key."

The best advice, on the whole, is that of the Arabic proverb, "Marry the girl of a good family though she be seated on a mat, very poor."

Again, there is an old saying, "Go down the ladder when thou marriest a wife; go up when thou choosest a friend;" for, as another proverb explains it, "Marry above your match and you get a master." This is undoubtedly true, and, as they say in France, "Who taketh a wife for her dower turns his back on freedom;" the Spanish equivalent being, "In the rich woman's house she commands always and he never."

In the choice of a wife, it has long been proverbially held that matrimony has the most chance of success where equals join with equals, or, as the well-known adage expresses it, "Like blood, like good, like age, make the happiest marriages." And there is the Italian saying, "Take a vine of a good soil and a daughter of a good mother."

And, since in marriage "A man hath tied a knot with his tongue that he cannot untie with all his teeth," he is enjoined to be wise, and "in wiving and thriving to take counsel of all the world;" and in an old work, entitled "The Countryman's New Commonwealth," published in 1647, this advice is given:—

> "In choice of a virtue let virtue be thy guide,
> For beauty's a blossom that fadeth like pride;
> And wealth without wisdom will waste far away:
> If chaste thoughts be lacking, all soon will decay."

Among further items of proverbial wisdom we are told that, in the choice of a woman, "It is better to marry a quiet fool than a witty scold," although, according to another adage, "It is better to marry a shrew than a sheep"—a sheep being a woman without individuality or will of her own—a nonentity. Thus, in the old play of "Tom Tyler and his Wife," one of the songs says :—

> "To marry a sheep, to marry a shrew,
> To meet with a friend, to meet with a foe :
> These checks of chance can no man flie
> But God Himself that rules the skie."

And when it is remembered that—

> "The best or worst thing to Man for his life,
> Is good or ill—choosing his good or ill wife"—

it is no matter of surprise that he is warned to be prudent, for, as the old proverb already quoted runs—

> "Who weds ere he be wise,
> Shall die ere he thrive."

Chinese folk-lore contains much proverbial wisdom relative to women and marriage, much of which, if not always instructive, is amusing. Thus, it is said, "If heaven wants to rain, or your mother to marry again, nothing can prevent them ;" and, according to a popular rhyme—

> "In the great majority of cases,
> Wives have fair and husbands ugly faces ;
> Yet there are many on the other side
> Where the man is bound to an ugly bride."

Again, it is said, "A talented bridegroom is sometimes married to a worthless bride, and a clever woman is sometimes matched with a dolt"—an aphorism, indeed, which is found in the proverbial literature of most countries ; a Hindustani proverb warning the fair sex that "A clever maid married to a fool sorrows." On the other hand, when a young girl is about to be married, if the family on either side is agreeable to the union of the two, it is considered a matter for congratulation, for, as the Chinese proverb runs—

> "Marriages, when properly negotiated,
> Cause neither family to be aggravated ;"

and, on this account, a young lady's parents are thus enjoined :—

> "In betrothing a daughter to any young man,
> Very careful inquiry's the only safe plan ;"

or, as another version has it, "In marrying a daughter select an excellent son-in-law," and the reason for taking this precaution is given in another admonitory proverb :—

> "The bride that is linked to a worthless groom
> Is like a man buried in a luckless tomb."

And, it may be added, it is also said, "In marrying a son seek a virtuous maiden, and scheme not for a rich dowry."

The bait of money as an inducement to matrimony has always been condemned, for, as the Dutch say—

> "Who weds a sot to get his lot,
> Will lose the cot and get the sot."

But perhaps some of the strictest warnings are

to be found in the Sanskrit folk-tales and proverbs, in which only too often women are pictured in a far from favourable light, one reason, we are told, being that even marriage does not satisfy a woman's vanity, which is never satisfied. Accordingly, it is said, "The fire is never satisfied with the addition of fuel, the ocean with the influx of rivers, the Angel of Death with the mortality of all things which hath seen life, nor a beautiful woman with the conquest of all mankind;" and, it is added, "Women will forsake a husband who is possessed of every good quality—reputable, comely, good, obsequious, rich, and generous—to steal to the company of some wretch who is destitute of every accomplishment and virtue." And yet, however much the advisability of marriage, in most countries, may be questioned, the Chinese adage must be allowed to pass without contradiction:—

> "For wives your sons are longing, your maids for husbands call;
> This is the one arena in which strive one and all;"

to which may be added the Talmud proverb, which runs thus: "God did not make woman from man's head, that she should not rule over him; nor from his feet, that she should not be his slave; but from his side, that she should be near his heart;"[1] and, as it is said in Russian proverbial lore, "All meat is to be eaten, all maids to be wed."

[1] Cf. another Talmud proverb: "Women are parts cut out of men."

CHAPTER XVII

WOMEN AS WIVES

"Husband and wife in perfect accord are the music of the harp and lute."—*Chinese Proverb.*

"IN buying horses and taking a wife," runs an Italian proverb, "shut your eyes and commend yourself to God;" and, according to an old English proverb, "One should choose a wife with the ears rather than with the eyes," for "A man's best fortune, or his worst, is his wife;" whereas another Italian proverb says that if a man would be really happy he should "praise a wife but remain a bachelor."

The fact that, in all ages, the taking of a wife has been regarded as a hazardous blessing accounts for the numerous proverbial aphorisms on the subject; for, as the Scotch say:—

"The gude or ill hap o' a gude or ill life
Is the gude or ill choice o' a gude or ill wife;"

a further version of which runs as follows :—

> "Him that has a good wife no evil in life that may not be borne can befall,
> Him that has a bad wife no good thing in life can chance to, that good you may call ;"

the equivalent of which is found in China, "Negligent farming may induce temporary poverty, but a mistake in marrying blights a whole life." And there is another version, "When a man's vessel is upset and its masts broken, he is poor for a time ; but when a man marries a bad wife he is poor for life." Indeed, since the wife is the key of the house, he is by general consent a fortunate man who alights on a good one, for—

> "A little house well filled,
> A little land well tilled,
> And a little wife well willed
> Are great riches."

And again :—

> "Two things doth prolong this life,
> A quiet heart and a loving wife ;"

whereas a bad wife, as the Germans say, "is the shipwreck of her husband."

Under a variety of forms we find this folk-rhyme current in different parts of the country, and hence, it is said, "in choosing a wife and buying a sword, we ought not to trust another." And so rarely is a good wife, we are told, to be found that, to quote an old adage, "there is one good wife in the country, and every man thinks he has wed her." On this account—

> " Saith Solomon the wise,
> A good wife's a great prize."

It is also said that—

> " A good wife and a good name
> Hath no mate in goods nor fame."

And that—

> " A good wife and health
> Are a man's best wealth "—

the same idea being found in the Chinese proverb, "Good tempered and careful, she's a good wife indeed ;" two Eastern proverbs, on the other hand, reminding us that "A passionate wife is as bad as a house that leaks," and "Where there is discord it is the marriage of two corpses." Indeed, that a good wife is a man's best helpmate has been universally acknowledged, a popular proverb reminding us that "Good housewifery trieth to rise with the clock ;" whereas Tusser truly says, "Ill housewifery lieth till nine of the clock." Among similar proverbs, it is said in China that "the more a wife loves her husband the more she corrects his faults ;" and, on the other hand, according to a Spanish proverb, "The woman who has a bad husband makes a confidant of her maid." But when husband and wife love each other and work together, then, to quote a Dutch proverb—

> " When the husband earns well,
> The wife spins well."

And we may quote the Indian proverb, "A chaste wife is very bashful, and a bad one a great talker;" and there is the West Indian adage, "The husband's flour, the wife's salt," meaning that both should earn something.

On the other hand, a bad wife is the cause of a man's undoing, for it is "certain sorrow to bring a termagant wife into a house," such a man, says a Persian adage, "being tied by the neck, that is married to a bad woman;" and, as we read in "Proverbs of Hendyng":—

"Many a man singeth
When he home bringeth
His young wife:
Wist he what he brought,
Weep he mought,
Er his life syth,
Quoth Hendyng"—

the equivalent of which we find in an Eastern saying, "A virtuous wife causes her husband to be honoured, a bad one brings him to shame;" and there is the Hindustani adage, "The house that has a bad wife is on the eve of ruin;" the counterpart of which occurs in Proverbs xii. 4, "A virtuous woman is a crown to her husband, but she that maketh ashamed is as rottenness to his house." Equally significant is the Persian proverb which describes a bad wife as a tree growing on the wall, *i.e.*, like the fig tree, which undermines the wall by its roots.

And yet, if proverbial philosophy be true, "The calmest husbands make the stormiest wives."

But this evidently is not always the case, for "When the husband is fire and the wife tow, the devil easily sets them in flames." But there is truth in the Tamil proverb, which belongs also to other countries, "Husbands are in heaven whose wives chide not;" with which may be compared the Spanish adage, "It is a good horse that never stumbles, and a good wife that never grumbles." A good-looking wife, it would appear, is not always a blessing, for—

> "A fair wife, a wide house, and a back door
> Will quickly make a rich man poor."

She is supposed to need looking after, inasmuch as he "who hath a fair wife needs more than two eyes," and "he that hath a white horse and a fair wife never wants trouble." An African proverb reminds us that "He who marries a beauty marries trouble," with which may be compared the Spanish one, "A handsome wife brings no fortune;" and a Marathi proverb repeats the same warning, "A good-looking wife is the world's, an ugly one is our own." There is some truth in the Hindustani proverb, "God protects the blind man's wife," for he cannot look after her and control her movements. Hence the warning, "Commend not your wife, wine, nor house," for fear of undue advantage being taken of the confidence reposed in another. The Chinese, on the other hand, whilst discountenancing a good-looking wife as a blessing, have this proverb, "Ugly wives and stupid maids are priceless treasures," for there is no chance of any one running away with them; with which may be classed the German adages, "The blind man's wife needs no paint," and "A deaf husband and a blind wife are always a happy couple." The danger of a man meddling with another man's wife—whatever the temptation offered him—has been handled in the proverbial lore of most countries, a good illustration being that contained in Hindustani maxims :—

> "Better catch a serpent and suck poison,
> Than have dealings with another's wife;"

and another Hindustani proverb warns us that "A fool's wife is every one's sister-in-law," implying that any one may flirt with her;[1] whilst a West Indian proverb speaks of "another's wife as a poisonous plant." Proverbial wisdom, too, would seem to be universally agreed that no man but a fool trusts his wife to another's care, and a Marathi maxim enjoins the husband thus: "Tie up and carry with you your wife and your money;" for, as a Hindustani adage warns us, "A shameless wife dances at others' houses." But according to another Eastern proverb, "That wife is best who never goes to another's house, and fears her husband as the cow fears the butcher;" for, as it is also said, "Women and children get lost by wandering from house to house."

There is a danger, too, lest a fair wife should be vain, and neglect her household duties, passing

[1] See Fallon's "Hindustani Proverbs."

her time in seeking the admiration of the outside world, for "A woman that loves to be at the window is like a bunch of grapes on the highway." A good wife, said the wisdom of our forefathers, "is to be from her house three times: when she is christened, married, and buried," a mode of life, we are afraid, somewhat difficult of attainment. But, at any cost, the prudent man is warned by a host of proverbs that—

> "A window wench, and a trotter in street,
> Is never good to have a house to keep."

A wife, too, of this stamp is only too frequently idle, and indifferent to everything save their own personal attractions; and where the home is of not much account this is all the more noticeable. Hence the adage says, "Bare walls make giddy housewives," upon which Ray has this note: "Idle housewives, because they have nothing whereabout to busy themselves, and show their good housewifery. We speak this in excuse of the good woman, who doth, like St. Paul's widow, περιέρχεσθαι τὰς οἰκίας, gad abroad a little too much, or is blamed for not giving the entertainment that is expected, or not behaving herself as other matrons do. She hath nothing to look upon at home. She is disconsolate, and therefore seeketh to divert herself abroad; she is inclined to be virtuous, but discomposed through poverty. Parallel to this I take to be that French proverb, 'Vuides chambres font les dames folles,' which Cotgrave thus renders, 'Empty chambers make women play the wanton,' in a different sense." In Cheshire the peasantry, speaking of a young wife who grows idle after marriage, say, "She hath broken her elbow at the church door."

Such a wife, again, is occasionally apt to be untidy and slovenly in her habits :—

"Fair and sluttish, black and proud,
Long and lazy, little and loud ;"

or, as another version has it :—

"Fair and foolish, little and loud,
Long and lusty, black and proud ;
Fat and merry, lean and sad,
Pale and pettish, red and bad ;"

for "beauty and folly do often go hand in hand, and are often matched together." And yet, after all, it is said, "There's but an hour in the day between a good housewife and a bad, for, as Ray explains it, "With a little more pains, she that slatters might do things neatly." In other words :—

"The wife that expects to have a good name,
Is always at home as if she were lame ;
And the maid that is honest, her chiefest delight
Is still to be doing from morning to night ;"

which also has been expressed, "The foot on the cradle and the hand on the distaff is the sign of a good housewife." According to an old proverb, "An obedient wife commands her husband, which has its parallel in Scotland, where one may often hear the remark, "A wife is wise enough when she kens her gudeman's breeks frae her ain kirtle," which has been thus explained, "She is a good wife who knows the true measure of her husband's authority and her obedience"—a proverb which is just the reverse of the Arabian one, "The wife wears the breeches;" or, as we should say, she rules her husband. But it is generally agreed, to quote the German adage, that "There is nothing worse on earth than when the wife becomes the master," an evil which is invariably the case when a poor man marries a wealthy woman, for, as they say in Spain, "In the rich woman's house she always commands, he never." And there is the Marathi proverb to the same effect: "She manages well whose husband is a slave to her;" and another, "If the wife is bigger than the husband she will run after him with the pestle." There is, too, a similar Hindustani proverb spoken of a henpecked husband, "A man in the power of a woman dances to her like a donkey;" to which is added the warning, "Check your wife and she'll make you suffer," a further adage describing the henpecked husband as "his own wife's pupil." It is generally agreed that no greater misfortune can happen to a man than to have a wife his master, for, as a Welsh proverb which has been aptly translated tells us—

"The rule of a wife,
A daughter's ill-life,
A son that is an untaught clown
May turn the whole world upside down";

another one telling us that "Three things no credit to their owners yield, a ruling wife, lean horse, and barren field." And the German adage even goes so far as to say that, in such a case, "a man must ask his wife's leave to thrive."

An old name for a hen-pecked husband was "John Tomson's man," the phrase having been used by Dunbar, who, in one of his petitions to James IV. for preferment, expresses the wish that his Majesty might for once be "John Tomson's man," the Queen being favourable to the poet's suit; and the term applied to a husband whose wife rules the roost is still "a woman's kingdom."

Although a wife's wisdom is not estimated at a very high value, the husband is enjoined not to disregard it, for, as the proverb says, "A woman's counsel is not worth much, but he that despises it is no better than he should be." The reason for this advice is, as the Germans say, "that summer-sown corn and women's advice turn out well once in seven years,"[1] and, on this account, the opportunity, however remote, of its proving advantageous should not be thrown away. A Servian proverb says that "It is sometimes right even to obey a sensible wife," in illustration of which Kelly gives the following humorous little anecdote:[2] A Herzegovinian once asked a kadi whether a man ought to obey his wife, whereupon the kadi answered that there was no

[1] See Chapter on "Women's Characteristics."
[2] "Proverbs of all Nations."

occasion to do so. The Herzegovinian then continued, "My wife pressed me this morning to bring thee a pot of beef suet, so I have done well in not obeying her." Then said the kadi, "Verily, it is sometimes right even to obey a sensible wife."

We find various qualifications, however, in the matter of following a wife's counsel, one proverb saying, "Take your wife's first advice, not her second," the reason assigned being that "Women are wise offhand, and fools on reflection." But perhaps the best rule is this, "In the husband wisdom, in the wife gentleness," for it is said, according to the Talmud maxim, "Even though thy wife be little, bow down to her in speaking;" in other words, be kind to her and do nothing without her advice; and the Chinese have a proverb much to the same effect:—

> "A good man will not beat his wife,
> A good dog will not worry a fowl."

And the Russian proverb tells us that the wife ought to be treated with due respect, for "She is not a guitar, which, having done playing with, the husband hangs on the wall." An Eastern proverb offers different advice when it says, "Beat a bullock every other furrow, and a wife every other day."

According to a popular adage, "Wife and children are bills of charge," and "A fair wife without a fortune is a fine house without furniture;" and, on the other hand, it is said that "A poor man's wife is always underrated."

It is frequently said, too, that an extravagant wife makes even a rich man poor, which reminds us of the gipsy's rhyme :—

"A man may spare,
And still be bare,
If his wife be nowt, if his wife be nowt ;
But a man may spend,
And have money to lend,
If his wife be owt, if his wife be owt."

But there is the reverse side of the picture, an illustration of which we may take from Hindustani proverbial lore, which, speaking of the extravagant husband, says, "My lord is a dandy abroad, but at home there is a dragged tailed wife ;" "Abroad my lord goes in gorgeous array, with a naked wife at home ;" and "Abroad he is my lord governor, at home lies a victim of fate," that is, "she is a poor, miserable creature." But when a man is rich, and is liberal to his wife, the case is different, for a world-wide adage says, "A rich man's wife is always respected ;" and hence "A house well furnished makes a good housewife." Gossiping wives are to be avoided, for, as an Eastern proverb says, "The gadding wife will see a snake in the fire," that is, will make any excuse to run out ; and as the Yorkshire peasantry are wont to say, "A rouk-town's seldom a good housewife at home," a "rouk-town" being a nickname for a gossiping housewife who spends her time in going from house to house. Similarly, there is a Sinhalese proverb to this effect, "You must get a talkative wife if you wish to receive slaps on the face from every one," for she is sure, sooner or later, to make mischief; and an old English proverbial phrase reiterates the same warning:—

> "A young wife and a harvest goose,
> Much cackle will both;
> A man that hath them in his clos [possession]
> He shall rest wroth." [1]

The Chinese say, "A young wife should be in her house but a shadow and an echo." And this trait of woman's character is viewed in no favourable way in proverbial lore, for a Suffolk aphorism defines a young lady who is over inquisitive as being "fond of gape-seed," that is, staring at everything that passes.

Incidental allusions have been made to indiscreet selection of wives, and it is said that he who marries for love without money will have good nights and sorry days; and, on the other hand, the following folk-rhyme tells only too often the experience of many:—

> "Sorrow and an evil life,
> Maketh soon an old wife."

According to another rhyme, we are told how he—

> "Who builds his house of sallows,
> And pricks his blind horse over the fallows,
> And suffereth his wife to go seek hallows,
> Is worthy to be hanged on the gallows."

[1] MS. of fifteenth century in "Relig. Antiq.," ii. 113, quoted by W. Carew Hazlitt, "English Proverbs and Proverbial Phrases," 1869, p. 41.

And once more :—

> "He that hath a good neighbour hath a good morrow,
> He that hath a shrewd wife hath much sorrow,
> He that fast spendeth must needs borrow,
> But when he must pay again there is all the sorrow."

A man who takes to himself a wife is warned against expecting that he will have nothing but success, for, as it is said—

> "A man may not wive,
> And also thrive,
> And all in a year."

That the wife who has a grievance will be sure to make it known is exemplified in such adages as the following : "She that marries ill never wants something to say for it ;" or, as another one puts it, "She that hath an ill husband shows it in her dress ;" and again, "Women, priests, and poultry have never enough." There are many curious folk-rhymes of a descriptive character, of which the following is a specimen :—

> "A baker's wife may bite of a bun,
> A brewer's wife may drink of a tun,
> A fishmonger's wife may feed of a conger,
> But a serving man's wife may starve for hunger."

Among some of the many other wise sayings, we are told in Scotland, "Better the mother wi' the pock than the faither wi' the Jack," the meaning being, says Kelly, that "the mother, though in a low condition, will be more kindly to, and more careful of, orphans, than the father can be, though in a better." And yet, after all, despite all their faults :—

> "Wives must be had,
> Be they good or bad."

For, as the Chinese say, "Husband and wife in perfect concord are like the music of the harp and lute ;" and again, "A man without a wife has a home without a mistress ; and a woman without a husband is an unprotected being ;" or, as another version has it, "A woman without a husband is like the sand of the river," the German form being, "A woman without a husband, a house without a foundation." It is, too, further said that "The beauty of a woman without a husband is in vain ;" and conversely, "A man without a wife is a house without a roof." There are many forms of this proverbial piece of wisdom, the following being found among Hindustani proverbs : "Without a wife the house doth howl ;" "Without a wife the house is the abode of the devil ;" but "With a wife the house doth joy ;" and "the death of the wife is ruin to the house ;" and, once more, "With the housewife the house is lively, without the housewife the house is dull ;" and, according to a Marathi proverb, "The husband is the life of the woman."

Some of the proverbial experiences relative to second wives are amusing and instructive, an old maxim observing that "the man who has taken one wife deserves a crown of patience, the man who has taken two deserves two crowns of pity ;" but a German proverb takes a different view, "A man who marries a second time deserves not to have lost his first wife," and adds, "To marry once a duty, twice a folly, thrice it's madness."

Spanish lore tells us that "the first wife is a broom, the second a lady;" which is much the same as the German adage, "the first wife is a servant, the second a lady." Among Kashmiri proverbs, too, we find much the same opinion expressed :—

> "The first wife is as jasmine and income;
> The second wife swears hourly by your name;[1]
> The third wife cuts bridges, great and small;[2]
> The fourth wife—there is no one like her for all manner of wickedness. She is a hopeless character."[3]

The Italians, who have an extensive collection of proverbs relating to the choice of wives, many of which are very humorous, say that "the first wife is matrimony, the second company, the third heresy;" and in Germany a young wife is often reminded of the proverb, "The jealousy of the wife is the path to divorce."

It was a popular belief that the features of those who have been long married assimilate, and become like each other—a pretty idea thus described by the late Lord Tennyson :—

> "But that God bless thee, dear—who wrought
> Two spirits to one equal mind,
> With blessings beyond hope or thought,
> With blessings which no words can find;"

[1] Makes great professions of love.
[2] Mischievous and extravagant.
[3] See J. H. Knowles, "Kashmiri Proverbs," 1885.

and which Sir Walter Scott, in his "Lay of the Last Minstrel," has thus noticed :—

> "It is the secret sympathy,
> The silver link, the silken tie,
> Which heart to heart, and mind to mind,
> In body and in soul can bind" —

a widespread fragment of folk-lore which has found its way into many an old romance and legendary tale; and a further pretty illustration of which we quote from Moore's "Loves of the Angels" :—

> "Whose hearts in every thought are one,
> Whose voices utter the same wills,
> Answering, as echo doth, some tone
> Of fairy music 'mong the hills,
> So, like myself, we seek in vain
> Which is the echo, which the strain."

And we may quote the Spanish adage, "Observe the face of the wife to know the husband's character;" and contrariwise a Marathi proverb puts it, the most important point in home-life is the character of the wife, for "if the wife be sensible there will be good management, if not there will be ruin." And again, the Hindu proverb, of which there are sundry versions elsewhere, says, "patience, rectitude, friend, and wife, all four are tested by calamity," for, speaking of the average wife, it is added, "She loves and she serves, but in the time of need she's off."

CHAPTER XVIII

YOUNG AND OLD MAIDS

"The hand of time alone disarms
Her face of its superfluous charms,
But adds for every grace resigned,
A thousand to adorn her mind."

BROOME.

THERE is a wide difference between the young girl about to enter life, and the middle-aged spinster soured by disappointed hopes, and hence the Hindustani proverb asks, "What is the good of mincing when you are growing old?" Some allowance must be made for the petulancy and coquetry of youth, and an old adage of proverbial philosophy has perhaps saved many an inexperienced swain from marrying a penniless girl barely out of the schoolroom, by whispering in his ear, "Sweetheart and honeybird keeps no house;" and although the spirit of chivalry has always prompted mankind to see nothing but good in maidenhood, yet a Spanish proverb has boldly put this question, "All are good maids, but whence come the bad wives?" which the proverbial lore of our own and other countries has wisely left unanswered.[1]

Girlhood, as it has been often said, is fleeting and fragile; and, according to a Scotch proverb, "Glasses and lasses are brackle [brittle] wares." Another piece of Scotch folk-lore referring to the transitoriness of youth, says that "Lassies are like lamb-legs; they'll neither saut nor keep;" whereas Hindustani lore tells us that "Maidenhood is perennial spring."

If we may credit the verdict of our forefathers, a characteristic of inexperienced girlhood is doing the very thing which is declared to be impossible. Thus, it is said, "Maids say nay and take"—a kiss, a ring, or an offer of marriage. A similar adage, says Mr. Jeaffreson,[2] "'The maid that taketh yieldeth,' was often quoted in old time by the pedantical jurists, who declared that by taking a ring a girl yielded to the entreaties of her suitor even to the point of becoming his spouse."

Her hesitancy, too, has usually placed her at the mercy of her pursuer. "The maid that laughs," says proverbial lore, "is half taken;" and it takes care to add, "the woman that wavers is lost."

Many a young girl, we are told, loses her opportunity of marriage through either not being able to make up her mind, or owing to her not being satisfied with one sweetheart, hence the saying, "A lass that has many wooers oft fares the worst."

[1] See Chapter on "Woman's Goodness."
[2] "Brides and Bridals," i. p. 349.

As might be expected, the wise saws of old had much to say about the treatment of young ladies, and according to a well-known Scotch proverb, "Maidens should be mim till they're married, and then they may burn kirks," which Kelly thus explains: "Spoken often by way of reflection, when we say that such an one is a good-humoured girl, as if you would say, 'Observe how she'll prove when she is married.'"

The monitor, it has been observed, had some true knowledge of human nature, who, "for the benefit of lads pursuing jealously-guarded damsels," produced the couplet :—

"He that would the daughter win,
Must with her mother first begin ;"

or, as another version has it, "Daughters and dead fish are no keeping wares," implying that daughters should be married and dead fish eaten, otherwise they will both spoil in the hands of their possessors. But, on the other hand, mothers are reminded that it is far from an easy thing always to find a husband for her daughter, hence it is said, "Marry your son when you will, your daughter when you can," an admonition, indeed, which explains the following: "Marriageable foolish wenches are troublesome troops to keep." It is further added, "Marry your daughters betimes, lest they marry themselves."

There would seem to be some art in courting a fair maiden, for "he that woos a maid must feign, lie, and flatter," whereas another proverb says,

"He that woos a maid must come seldom in her sight," or, in other words, he must avoid excess of eagerness in courting, for—

> "Follow love, and it will flee,
> Flee love, and it will follow thee."

But, on the other hand, it must not be forgotten that—

> "Lad's love is lassie's delight,
> And if lads won't love, lassies will flite"

—*flite* meaning to scold, the same as the Scottish *flit.*

Daughters, it is said, generally take after their mothers, "Like mother, like daughter," although there are many exceptions to this rule, for an old proverb says, "A light heel'd mother makes a heavy heel'd daughter," because she does all the work herself, and her daughter in the meantime sitting idle, contracts a habit of sloth. Similarly in France we find the same idea, "Mère pitieuse fait sa fille rogneuse"—"A tender mother makes a scabby daughter."

From time immemorial the old maid has been made an object of ridicule, and the only thing according to proverbial folk-lore that she is fit for is to "lead apes in hell":—

> "And now, Tatlanthê, thou art all my care:
> Pity that you, who've served so long and well,
> Should die a virgin, and lead apes in hell.
> Choose for yourself, dear girl, our Empire round,
> Your portion is three hundred thousand pound."

Shakespeare makes Katherine say to her father in allusion to Bianca :—

> "She is your treasure, she must have a husband.
> I must dance barefoot on her wedding-day,
> And for your love to her lead apes in hell."

Malone, on this passage, remarks that in olden times "to lead apes" was one of the employments of a bear-ward, who often carried about one of those animals along with his bear. It was also customary, in days gone by, for elder sisters to dance barefooted at the marriage of a younger one, as otherwise they would inevitably become old maids.

In different parts of the country, too, a custom once practised was that of the elder sister dancing in a hog's trough in consequence of the younger sister marrying before her—when it was considered the most correct thing to dance in green stockings.

"In Spain," writes Mr. Finck, "old maids are rare, because a girl generally accepts her first offer, and there are probably not many girls who do not receive at least one offer in their life. In Russia a curious custom prevails whereby a girl of uncertain age may escape the appellation of old maid. She may leave home and become lost for two or three years in Paris, London, or some other howling wilderness of humanity. Then she may return to her friends neither as maid nor wife, but as a widow. And it is good form in Russian Society to accept this myth without asking for details."

In Scotland there is a time-honoured adage, "Oh for a drap o' gentle blude, that I may wear black abune my brow," which shows that an old maid fares worse there than elsewhere. "In Scotland," writes Kelly, "no woman is suffered to wear a silk hood unless she be a gentlewoman, that is, a gentleman's daughter, or married to a gentleman. A rich maid having the offer of a wealthy yeoman, or a bare gentleman, wished for the last to qualify her to wear a black hood. It is since spoken to such wealthy maidens upon the like occasion."

Some allowance must be made for old maids if they are proverbially sour and crabby—"As spiteful as an old maid," as the phrase goes—and apt to speak in a disparaging manner of their younger sisters. Thus, in Scotland and the North of England, one may often hear some prim spinster remark, "Lassies nowadays ort nae God's creatures"—this being, says Jamieson, "the proverbial reflection of an old woman, as signifying that in our times young women are by no means nice in their choice of husbands."

But it only too often happens that the old maid tries to appear juvenile, and hence in Lancashire, when inquiries respecting the health of an absent friend are made, the subjoined couplet is frequently quoted by way of reply:—

"Quite young and all alive,
Like an old maid of forty-five."

There comes, however, a time when such frolicsome ways have to be abandoned, and then it is said of a woman, when there is no disguising her age, "This maid was born old."

But, however much old maids may be exposed to undeserved ridicule, many a piece of romance tells how invariably such a fate is due to no fault of their own, as is instanced by the following traditionary tale :—

"Years ago some Welsh miners, in exploring an old pit that had long been closed, found the body of a young man dressed in a fashion long out of date. The peculiar action of the air of the mine had been such as to preserve the body so perfectly that it appeared asleep rather than dead.

"The miners were puzzled at the circumstance ; no one in the district had been missed within their remembrance ; and at last it was resolved to bring the oldest inhabitant—an old lady, long past her eightieth year, who had lived single in the village the whole of her life. On being brought into the presence of the body, a strange scene occurred ; the old lady fell on the corpse, kissed, and addressed it in every term of loving endearment, couched in the quaint language of a bygone generation. 'He was her only love ; she had waited for him during her long life ; she knew that he had not forsaken her.'

"The old woman and the young man had been betrothed sixty years before. The lover had disappeared mysteriously, and she had kept faithful during that long interval. Time had stood still with the dead man, but had left its mark on the living woman. The miners who were present were a rough set ; but very gently, and with tearful eyes, they escorted the old lady to her house, and the same night her faithful spirit rejoined that of her long-lost lover."

And it must be remembered that, after all the severe judgment which has been passed by cynical proverbial lore on old maids, much has been said in their favour ; for, according to a Bengal adage, "A clever woman is not old, though aged, but has the sweet sap of wit in her ;" and a Sinhalese saying reminds us that, whatever its surroundings, and wherever found, "A gem is a gem ;" and yet, according to Hindustani [1] proverbial lore, "An old maid is a pack of evil."

[1] See Fallon's "Hindustani Proverbs."

CHAPTER XIX

WIDOWS

> "May widows wed as often as they can,
> And ever for the better change their man;
> And some devouring plague pursue their lives
> Who will not well be govern'd by their wives."
>
> DRYDEN'S *Wife of Bath.*

WIDOWS, who have been described in a Chinese proverb as so many rudderless boats, have had at all times the reputation of being dangerous; and proverbial philosophy has been more or less severe on them, an oft-quoted German maxim affirming that "Women lose their husbands, but they worship their bonnets." Hindustani proverbial lore inculcates much the same lesson: "The husband dead, and she continues to dress her hair;" and another oft-quoted maxim telling how, "Forgetting the olden time, the widow is bearing a marriage chaplet," in other words, making a display of herself, and which, we are told, in a wider sense, is commonly applied to those who in prosperity have forgotten the meanness of their origin.[1] On the other hand, the widows who frequently make the greatest display of sorrow are said to be those who are indifferent to their husband's happiness when alive, a fact which is noticed even in a Marathi proverb: "While he was alive she was not affectionate, now he is dead she breaks her necklaces and bangles"; and another Marathi proverb warns us that for a new husband a woman's love lasts nine days, and for a dead one only three days. According to Charles Mackay, in his "Safe Predictions"—

> "Whene'er you see a widow weeping
> In public sight,
> And still in flagrant notice keeping
> Her doleful plight,
> Aye talking of her dear departed;
> One truth is plain,
> She will not languish broken-hearted,
> But wed again";

for, as the Spanish proverb says, "A buxom widow must be either married, buried, or shut up in a convent;" and, as the Marathi adage adds, "Neither hair nor anything yet a widow is attractive." In an old piece of proverbial wisdom a man is strictly enjoined to keep himself "from the anger of a great man, from the tumult of a mob, from a man of ill fame, from a widow that has been thrice married, from wind that cometh in at a hole, and from a reconciled enemy;" and an old Chinese proverb warns us how "Slanders cluster round a widow's door."

[1] See S. W. Fallon's "Hindustani Proverbs."

There are very many reasons given for not marrying a widow, especially when she may happen to have daughters; for "He that marries a widow and two daughters marries three stark thieves;" or, as another version has it, "He that marries a widow and two daughters has three back doors to his house." The same notion largely prevails on the Continent, and the Spanish say, "He that marries a widow and three children marries four thieves," the idea, of course, being that his wife will put away, as Kelly says, "things to them, or for them." Under one form or another we find the same piece of proverbial wisdom in most countries, and a common Hindustani adage reminds the man who is fascinated by a widow that, as a rule, "there is very little in the widow's pocket."

Again, it is said that "he who marries a widow will often have a dead man's head thrown in his dish;" and on this account, according to the old adage, "Never marry a widow unless her first husband was hanged," as in this case there will be little likelihood of her sounding his praises.

But, unfortunately for widows, they have generally been considered of a more or less designing turn of mind, oftentimes, however, in the freshness of their grief, making resolutions which afterwards they are only too eager to break. Thus, Voltaire, in one of his romances, represents a disconsolate widow vowing that she will never marry again "so long as the river flows by the side of the hill." But a few months afterwards she recovers from her loss, and, contemplating matrimony, takes counsel with a clever engineer. He sets to work, the river is deviated from its course, and in a short time it no longer flows by the side of the hill. The lady, released from all her good intentions, does not allow many days to elapse before she exchanges her weeds for a bridal veil.

Improbable as this little romance may seem, a veritable instance was recorded not so very long ago: A Salopian parish clerk, seeing a woman crossing the churchyard with a bundle and a watering can, followed her, curious to know what her intentions might be, and he discovered that she was a widow of a few months' standing. Inquiring what she was going to do with the watering can, she replied that she was about to sow some grass seed on her husband's grave, and had brought a little water to make it spring up quickly. The clerk told her there was no occasion to trouble; the grave would be green in good time.

"Ah! that may be," she answered; "but my poor husband made me promise not to marry again until the grass had grown over his grave, and having a good offer, I do not wish to break my promise, or keep as I am longer than I can help."

But many widows, it would seem, do not care to wait so long a time, for the adage runs that "A good time for courtship is when the widow returns from the funeral;" and, as another version has it, "Marry a widow before she leaves mourning;" or, as the Germans say, "Woo the widow whilst she is in weeds"—proverbial philosophy which would seem to illustrate the popular maxim that " Few women turn grey because their husbands die." Indeed, if there be any truth in the old proverb, " The tears of a young widow lose their bitterness when wiped by the hands of love ; " or, as the German proverb puts it, " The rich widow's tears soon dry ; " and another, " A rich widow weeps with one eye and laughs with the other." The man, however, who is fascinated by a widow's charms is recommended to bear this couplet in mind—

> " He that woos a maid must seldom come in sight,
> But he that woos a widow must woo her day and night "—

which is contrary to the generally received maxim, " A woman is like your shadow : follow her, she flies ; fly from her, she follows."

The best thing, of course, according to proverbial philosophy, is to avoid widows ; and, like Mr. Tony Weller, who marries a widow, landlady of the " Marquis of Granby," it says : " Sam, beware of the widders ; " and yet it would appear to be the chief function of a well-endowed widow to enrich landless younger sons, and in " The Contention " the wife says to the lady in black—

> " Go, widow, make some younger brother rich,
> And then take thought and die, and all is well."

Some of the common deceits of a widow are enumerated by Sir John Davies in his portrait of a widow, who, because she was incapable of them, is mentioned among the "Twelve Wonders of the World":—

> "My husband knew how much his death would give me,
> And therefore left me wealth to comfort and relieve me;
> Though I no more will have, I must not love disdain,
> Penelope herself did lovers entertain—
> And yet to draw on such as are of best esteem,
> Nor younger than I am, nor richer, will I seem."

Our forefathers were wont to affirm that "'Tis dangerous marrying a widow because she hath cast her rider," which reminds us of Gay's fable—

> "Why are those tears? Why droops your head?
> Is, then, your other husband dead?
> Or does a worse disgrace betide—
> Hath no one since his death applied?"

The following folk-doggerel, which will be found in the "Reliquiæ Hearnianæ" (215) and is called by Stowe "an old proverb," gives an oftentimes true and pathetic description of the wretched condition of a widow—

> "Women be forgetful,
> Children be unkind,
> Executors be covetous,
> And take what they find:
> If anybody asks where
> The dead's good become?
> They answer—
> So God me help and holydoom,
> He died a poor man."

À propos of this quaint rhyme, we may quote the subjoined extract from Weaver's "Funeral Monuments" (1631, p. 19): "As well heires as executors oftentimes inter both the honour and memory of the defunct together with his corps, perfidiously forgetting their fidelity to the deceased—of which it will please you read this old inscription depicted upon a wall within St. Edmund's Church, in Lombard Street, London :—

"Man the behovyth oft to have yis in mind,
Yat thow geveth wyth yin hond, yat sall thou fynd ;
For widowes be sloful, and chyldren beth unkynd,
Executors beth covetos, and kep al yat yey fynd.
If eny body ask wher the deddys goodys becam ?
Yey ansywer
So God me help and halidam, he died a poor man."

According to a Chinese proverb, "A maid marries to please her parents ; a widow to please herself ;" and it is said that—

"Mandarins, customers, and widow folk,
You must be careful not to provoke."

There may be some difference of opinion respecting the following : "Happy the wife who dies before her husband ; unhappy she who dies after him" ; the reason assigned being that "A widow is a rudderless boat." Among further items of Eastern proverbial wisdom, it is said that—

"Widow marriage must always be
Consummated immediately"—

the reason for this being that otherwise the widow will demand a higher price, or accept some one else's higher offer. It is generally said, too, that the widow, through being more wide awake than a bride, not infrequently tries to improve her position when marrying a second time; and hence this proverb—

> "Having lost her first husband, again she's a bride;
> And so she gets higher at every stride."

Making every allowance, however, for a widow's position, we are reminded that, as "A good horse will not turn back to eat grass, a good wife will not marry a second husband," which is much to the same purport as the following: "A loyal minister will serve but one Prince; a virtuous woman but one husband."

CHAPTER XX

WOMAN'S CURIOSITY

"The over curious are not over wise."—MASSINGER.

ACCORDING to an old French proverb, "Curiosity is so nearly akin to craftiness, that it can disfigure the most handsome faces." Both history and social romance afford many a striking instance of the dangerous and fatal effects of over-inquisitiveness, for, according to a Spanish proverb, "No woman sleeps so soundly that the twang of the guitar will not bring her to the window."

Under a variety of forms the well-known tradition of "Peeping Tom" survives in our midst to-day, who, at any cost, would gain a glimpse of Lady Godiva, as she rode on her noble errand through the streets of Coventry, and nursery literature perpetuates the gruesome spectacle that was revealed to the curious maiden who, despite warning, persisted in prying into the forbidden chamber of Bluebeard.

But stories of this kind have their counterpart in our family folk-lore. Dalton Hill Head, for instance, once the property of the family of Hedley, of Newcastle, has a strange story associated with it. Some years ago a woman named Mary Henderson—a connection, it is said, of George Stephenson, the engineer, had charge of the house. The gardener lived close by and kept a mastiff called "Ball." Mysterious and uncanny tales seem to have been told of this house, and when Mary Henderson asked the gardener to lend her "Ball" as a protection, he specially warned her not to look into a certain closet in the house.

"Curiosity, however, prompted her to disregard his warning, for, said she, 'what can there possibly be that I should not see?' Hence to the cupboard she went, when, on entering it, she discovered to her horror a quantity of children's bones—some in hat-boxes and some wrapped in articles of clothing. She understood now the gardener's advice, and wondered what the meaning could be. With her companion 'Ball' she retired to rest, but was soon aroused by strange sounds of dancing and singing upstairs. Being a courageous woman, she determined to investigate the matter, but the dog was terrified and unwilling to accompany her. She accordingly took him in her arms and went round the house. As is usual in such cases, all was still and undisturbed, but an attic window stood open." Further particulars respecting this strange affair are wanting, neither are we informed whether the music and dancing were resumed on succeeding nights.

Many a story, again, of the tragic results of woman's curiosity has been recorded from time to time, more or less resembling the romance of George Lillo, entitled, "Fatal Curiosity." We are told how young Wilmot, supposed to have perished at sea, returns to this country, and in disguise pays a visit to his parents, with whom he deposits a casket.

But his mother, out of curiosity, opens the casket, and finding that it contains articles of great value, she agrees with her husband to murder its owner. Scarcely had they committed the fatal deed, when they discovered that it was their own son whom they had killed.

It would seem, too, that woman's curiosity has been equally distasteful to all beings of supernatural order, and it may be remembered how the fairies of our old ballads have frequently withdrawn their favours on this account from mortals. In a variety of cases, for instance, the treasures of some enchanted castle suddenly disappear, owing to the recipient's curiosity leading her to open a prohibited door. Such an act of disobedience is never allowed to pass with impunity, in most cases causing the inquisitive woman more or less personal injury. Oftentimes, also, in folk-tales and romance, curiosity is repaid by some unwelcome surprise, as in Grimm's tale of Fitcher's Bird, where the unhappy heroine finds, in a room which she was specially warned not to approach, the bodies of her sisters hacked in pieces.

Thus among the fairy tales in which woman's curiosity holds a prominent place, we are told how a young Welsh girl went one day to a hiring fair, where she was addressed by a gentleman dressed in black, who asked her if she would undertake the management of his children.

"Yes, she would gladly do so," was her reply.

Her new master made one condition, which was that she should be blindfolded before starting on their way to his home.

She consented, and on reaching their destination the handkerchief was removed from her eyes, when she found herself in a beautiful mansion, in the presence of a number of little children. These were put under her charge, her master at the same time presenting her with a box of ointment, which she was to put on their eyes, giving her strict injunctions always to wash her hands immediately after using it, and to be particularly careful never to let a bit of it touch her own eyes.

She obeyed his rules, and for a time was very happy in her new home, until one morning, when putting the ointment on the children's eyes, curiosity induced her to touch one corner of her own with it. But no sooner had she done so than the children appeared to her like so many little imps. Getting frightened, and anxious to leave what she felt was an uncanny place, she took the first opportunity of asking leave to go and see her friends, a request which was readily granted her. Accordingly, a handkerchief was put over her eyes, and she was escorted some distance towards the neighbourhood of her own home, where on her arrival she took care to remain.

Strange to say, many years afterwards, when

visiting the fair, she saw a man steal something from a stall, and with one corner of her eye she recognised her old master.

Unthinkingly she said, "How are you, Master? How are the children?"

He replied, "How did you see me?"

"With the corner of my eye," she replied. But from that moment she paid the long-deferred penalty for her curiosity, and became blind in her left eye, the sight of which she never recovered.

It has long been a common belief that it is highly dangerous for a young lady to display curiosity in all matters of ghostly import, and many a German household tale gives the most thrilling details of disobedience in this respect.

Stories, too, are told of young girls forecasting the future on the eve of their wedding day, and, through over curiosity, of their having a very different response to their inquiries from what they expected. Thus a certain damsel was warned against peeping into the looking-glass after she had performed various divinatory rites, but her curiosity led her to do so, whereupon she was horrified at seeing the figure of Death frowning at her.

In many an old family residence there is the mysteriously haunted room, "of which the atmosphere is supernaturally fatal to body and mind." Hence, should curiosity foolishly induce any one to enter a room of this description, the effects are generally said to be more or less serious. Some few years ago the case was reported of a young lady whose curiosity caused her, despite all advice, to go into such a haunted room, but, adds the account, "she saw, heard, and felt horror so intense that she went mad, and never recovered sanity enough to tell how or why."

And, whilst speaking of woman's curiosity, there is the well-known story of the Lady Freemason, who, in a perhaps unique way, paid the penalty for her inquisitiveness. The lady in question was the Honourable Elizabeth St. Leger, and her father Lord Doneraile—a very zealous Mason—held a warrant and occasionally opened a lodge at Doneraile House. On one occasion it appears that previous to the initiation of a candidate to the first steps of Masonry, Miss St. Leger—either by accident or design—happened to be in an apartment adjoining the one used as a lodge room. Hearing the voices of the Freemasons, she thought it a good opportunity to see this mystery, and making a hole in the wall—which at this time was undergoing some alterations—with her scissors she suceeeded in gaining a view unobserved of the first two steps of the mystic ceremony.

But, unfortunately for her curiosity, it had never occurred to her that there was no mode of egress except through the room where the Freemasons were assembled engaged in carrying out the concluding part of the second stage, and, as she stealthily opened the door, "there stood before her, to her dismay, a grim and surly tiler with his long sword unsheathed. Go forward she could not, and, panic-struck, her shriek alarmed the members of the lodge, who, finding that she had witnessed their proceedings," resolved, it is said, at once "to put the fair spectatress to death; but her life was spared on condition of her going through the remaining steps of the mystic ceremony she had unlawfully witnessed."

This young lady afterwards married Richard Aldworth, of Newmarket, and whenever a benefit was given at the theatres in Dublin or Cork, in aid of the Masonic Female Orphan Asylum, she walked at the head of the Freemasons with her apron and other insignia of Freemasonary, and sat in the front row of the stage-box. According to another version of this romantic story, Miss St. Leger concealed herself in an empty clock case, where she remained in her secret hiding-place for a considerable time, until, on being discovered secreted, she was compelled to become a member of the craft.

Another equally strange traditionary account of woman's curiosity—the punishment for which is a striking illustration of the arbitrary state of affairs in Scotland in former days—was that of the wife of a lord of the Sessions, Lord Grange. It was suspected that the lady had by some manner or other contrived to learn the contents of some state papers of great consequence, and for fear she should divulge anything she had learnt therein, she was privately conveyed to the island of St. Kilda by her husband and son, where, on her arrival, she was to be left to shift for herself, the two sailing back again without any one having the slightest knowledge of what had transpired.

The disappearance of Lady Grange soon became a matter of comment, and although every effort was made to ascertain the place of concealment, it was to no purpose. Years passed without anything being heard of her, until accidentally after her death, which took place at the end or thirty years, her melancholy and romantic fate was ascertained. Her isolated island home afforded no implements for writing, but anxious to let posterity have some facts of her sad and eventful life, she worked it on her muslin apron with her hair.

Further stories are to be found in family history and romance of the hardships and perils to which curiosity has subjected the indiscreet of the fair sex, this propensity having oftentimes subjected them to the most unenviable experiences. Truly, as it has been observed, "the over curious are not over wise," and to woman's curiosity may be added these warning words:—

> "Search not to find what lies too deeply hid;
> Nor to know things whose knowledge is forbid."

CHAPTER XXI

SISTER LEGENDS

"Nine maidens fair in life were they,
Nine maidens fair in death's last fray,
Nine maidens fair in fame alway,
The maidens of Glen of Ogilvy."
Scotch Ballad.

MANY interesting stories founded on the heroism and self-denying love of sisters are current in different parts of the country, and form an interesting chapter in the folk-lore of the fair sex.

A pretty tradition told of the building of Linton Church, of which there are one or two versions, has already been given in a previous chapter,[1] being only one of the numerous historic romances which in simple language tell of the beautiful sacrifice that in extreme emergency a sister's love has been ready, at one time or another, to make, and, as in this case, to save the brother's life.

These traditionary stories, too, are not confined

[1] See page 83, and "Church-Lore Gleanings."

to any one country, but are found on the Continent among the legendary romances associated with many of the sacred buildings; and, as it has been remarked, they form some of the most pleasing illustrations of woman's worth.

In a variety of ways such acts of devotion are said to have been displayed, their memory still surviving in the local legend. The Glen of Ogilvy, a romantic spot in the Vale of Strathmore, is the scene of the legend of the "Nine Maidens." It appears that far back in past years this glen was the chosen residence of St. Donivald and his nine daughters. They lived in the glen "as in a hermitage, labouring the ground with their own hands, and eating but once a day, and then but barley water and bread."

On the death of St. Donivald, after a long life of incessant toil, the sisters removed to Abernethy, and dying there they were buried at the foot of a large oak, much frequented by pilgrims up to the time of the Reformation. They were canonised as the "Nine Maidens," and many churches were dedicated to them throughout Scotland. One of these churches was that of Strathmartine, near Dundee, with which is connected the well-known tradition of the "Nine Maidens of Pitempan" being devoured by a serpent at the Nine Maiden Well in that parish. This legendary story has been commemorated in a ballad which tells how—

"Nine maidens were they spotless fair,
With silver skins, bright golden hair,
Blue-eyed, vermilion-cheeked, nowhere
Their match in Glen of Ogilvy."

After describing their many virtues and life of self-denial, the ballad relates how at their death there came to their grave from every land many a sorrowing pilgrim, for—

> "Nine maidens fair in life were they,
> Nine maidens fair in death's last fray,
> Nine maidens fair in fame alway,
> The maids of Glen of Ogilvy."

Another romantic folk-tale tells how four young orphan sisters agreed to fill the five lancets in the north transept of York Cathedral with memorial glass, in patterns taken from their embroidery frames, which they had long laid aside for sorrow, in remembrance of a dead sister. The story further adds that they are reported to have knelt and prayed until, one by one, they passed away, and were laid to rest in a common grave. Hence these lancets have been popularly designated the "Five Sisters."

But sometimes these sister legends commemorated tragic scenes in past years. At Ballybunnion, for instance, situated within a few miles from Kerry Head, is a cavern which is known by the Irish peasantry as the "Cave of the Seven Sisters." The scenery around is of the most romantic and wildest description, and on the brink of one of the precipices formed by the rugged cliffs are the remains of an old castle, said once upon a time to have been inhabited by a gallant chieftain, the father of seven beautiful daughters.

But the story goes that in an unlucky hour

a fatal attachment sprang up between these seven fair maidens and the captain and his six brothers belonging to a private ship. The father's anger at his daughters falling in love with men whom he considered enemies to his country was unbounded, and admitted of no mercy. All entreaties to preserve their lives were ineffectual, and, at the chieftain's command, the men were brought one by one to the edge of the precipice, and were hurled into the foaming flood beneath. What the fate of their unhappy sweethearts was the legend does not say.

According to another version of the same tradition one of the Northern sea-king's invaded Ballybunnion, and invested the chieftain, Bunnion, in his castle. The garrison was slain, and the chieftain, rather than that his nine daughters should fall into the hands of the victorious king, flung them, one after another, into the abyss. From this occurrence the cave has been popularly nicknamed "the Cave of the Nine."

Scattered here and there in different parts of the country we find certain curiously shaped stones named after sisters, in connection with which all kinds of legendary stories are associated. Thus in the parish of Gwendron, Cornwall, are nine "Moor Stones"—perpendicular blocks of granite, which have evidently been placed in their present position with much labour. According to local tradition they indicate the graves of nine sisters, whereas some say these stones are the metamorphosed remains of maidens who in all probability were changed into stone for some wicked profanation of the Sabbath day. As Mr. Hunt points out in his "Romances of the West of England" such monuments of impiety are to be met with in different parts of the country.

The undulation in the chalk cliffs between Seaford and Beachy Head are popularly known as the "Seven Sisters," a number which, it may be noted, occurs frequently in the boundary lists of Saxon charters as "Seven oaks," "Seven thorns."

Sometimes, it would seem, wrong acts were punished in a less material way than by their agents being turned into stone. Denton Hall, for instance, has long been reported to be tenanted by a spirit commonly called "Silky," whose history is not without a romantic past. There is some obscure and dark rumour of secrets strangely obtained and cruelly betrayed by a rival sister, ending in deprivation of reason and death. As a penalty for her sin, the betrayer haunts the scene of her crime.

Happily, however, if we are to believe legendary lore, the rivalry of sisters has occasionally resulted in good works. Thus the two churches of Allrighton and Donington, in Shropshire, which stand curiously near together, are of different styles and dates; but tradition says they were built by two sisters in a spirit of rivalry, and that this is the reason why Donington parish church is so far from any village, and so much in one corner of the parish.

A similar story is told of Cowthorne and

Withernsea churches, Yorkshire, which are popularly nicknamed in the neighbourhood the "Sister Churches." It is said that they were built by two sisters, who at first agreed that a single church would be sufficient for the adjoining manors, but they quarrelled as to the respective merits of a tower or spire, and finally each sister built her own church.

To quote a further case a local tradition represents Ormskirk Church, Yorkshire, as having been erected at the cost of two maiden sisters named Orm, but being unable to decide as to whether the church should have a tower, or a spire, they accommodated their differences by giving it both. Roby discredits the story, remarking that the old ladies might each "have had her way by building a tower and surmounting it by a spire."

Among the numerous other stories of a legendary character connected with sisters may be mentioned that known as the "Two Sisters of Beverley." According to Poulson, the historian of Beverley, there is in the south isle of the Minster an altar-tomb placed under a pinnacled canopy, but without any inscription to lead to a knowledge of the occupant, or occupants. Tradition, however, assigns it to the unmarried daughters of Earl Puch, who are said to have given two of the common pastures to the free men of Beverley. In Ingledew's "Ballads of Yorkshire" there is a legendary ballad relating to the mysterious appearance and disappearance of these ladies at the convent. It concludes by referring to their burial and relates how—

> " Side by side in the chapel fair,
>   Are the sainted maidens laid,
> With their snowy brow, and glossy hair,
>   They look not like the dead !
> Fifty summers have come and passed away,
> But their loveliness knoweth no decay."

Legends of the same kind are found on the Continent. Near Louvain there are three graves in which rest the remains of three pious sisters. Before their graves three clear springs are said to burst forth, which possess marvellous medicinal properties. In order to know whether a woman will live or die of her malady, it is customary to take a hood belonging to her and to lay it on the water. If it sinks no recovery is to be looked for ; if, on the other hand, it swims, the disease is curable. Many such stories are current, and the folk-tales, it may be added, of most countries are prolific in a host of incidents in which the acts of sisters are the principal feature.

CHAPTER XXII

BRIDES AND THEIR MAIDS

"The bloom or blight of all men's happiness."
BYRON'S *Bride of Abydos.*

ACCORDING to the time-honoured adage—

"My son is my son till he gets him a wife,
But my daughter's my daughter all the days of her life."

This may be so, but with few exceptions, the bride thinks differently; for, however great a gap her absence may make in the old home, her feelings are those expressed in the charming ballad of bygone days, which generally found its way into most old books sold at village fairs, and which portrays the folk-lore of the subject, as told by the simple, bright-hearted maiden—

"As I walked forth one May morning,
I heard a fair maid sweetly sing,
As she sat under a cow milking,
We will be married o' Sunday.

I said, pretty maiden, sing not so,
For you must tarry seven years or mo',
And then to church you may chance to go
All to be married o' Sunday.

Kind sir, quoth she, you have no skill ;
I've tarried two years against my will,
And I've made a promise, will I, or nill,
That I'll be married o' Sunday.

Next Saturday night 'twill be my care
To trim and curl my maiden hair,
And all the people shall say, Look here !
When I come to be married o' Sunday.

Then to the church I shall be led
By sister Nan and brother Ned,
With a garland of flowers upon my head,
For I'm to be married o' Sunday.

And in the church I must kneel down
Before the parson of our good town,
But I will not spoil my kirtle and gown
When I'm married o' Sunday."

There are plenty of old ballads of this kind, many of which have been preserved in chap-books, and these are interesting in so far as they depict the sentiments of the past. But an Eastern piece of proverbial wisdom represents what must be regarded as an almost universal truism—

"The bride that is linked to a worthless groom
Is like a man buried in a worthless tomb"—

her whole future happiness being dependent on her good or bad choice. Hence it is not surprising that, in most ages of the world's history, the position of a bride has been regarded as the most critical in her life ; and, on this account, it has been associated with a host of proverbial sayings and superstitious beliefs, numerous survivals of which remain in our midst to-day.

Occasionally, for instance, one may hear the expression, "She brides it"—that is, "She holds up her head haughtily," in reference to a proud woman—the allusion, of course, being to the disdainful bride who, on her marriage-day bore herself in a pompous manner, fully conscious of her own charms. On the other hand, there is the well-known saying, "She simpers like a bride on her wedding day," in allusion to the brides of old times who were bound, in courtesy, to smile on all who approached them.

When a bride happens to be unpopular, she is sent off with the following far from complimentary farewell—

> "Joy go with her and a bottle ot moss,
> If she never comes back she'll be no great loss,"

the term, "bottle of moss," being applied to a thing of no value.

Whereas, nowadays, it is customary for a young lady to speak of going to church "on her wedding day," formerly she spoke of "visiting the church porch" a practice which explains the meaning of the old Irish proverbial saying, "Ye're early with your orders, as the bride said at the church porch." The popular adage, too, "Blest is the bride that the sun shines on," had once a practical application, when marriages were celebrated in the church porch. A wet day on such an occasion was a serious matter, as our forefathers had none of the useful contrivances of modern times for preservation from rain.

Another proverbial phrase once in use was to this effect: "You make a muck hill on my trencher, quoth the bride"—that is, "you carve me a great heap." According to Hazlitt, this saying probably originated "in some bride at first, thinking to speak elegantly and finely, using this expression, and so it was taken up in drollery, or else it was only a droll, made to abuse country bride affecting fine language."

It is still often said that "many dressers put the bride's dress out of order," her friends being over anxious to give it the finishing touch. Likewise, the bride herself when once her toilet is complete, must, according to a piece of folk-lore current in the Southern Counties, refrain from taking a last look in the glass, the idea being that the young lady who is too fond of the looking-glass will be unlucky when married; and in removing her robe and chaplet she must take care to throw away every pin worn on the eventful day, as evil fortune will inevitably overtake the bride who keeps even one pin used in the marriage toilet. Hence it is the duty of the bridesmaids to use every precaution that no pin is even accidently left in any part of her dress. Woe, also, to the bridesmaids if they retain any one of them, as their chances of marriage will thereby be materially diminished.

On the other hand, according to a Sussex piece of folk-lore, a bride, on her return home from church, is often at once robbed of all the pins about her dress by her single friends around her, from the belief that whoever possesses one of them will be married in the course of a year. Similarly, the Germans have a custom of throwing the bride's shoe among the guests at a wedding, the person who succeeds in getting it being considered to have every prospect of a speedy marriage ; and, among the many other customs associated with the bride's shoe, may be mentioned the German practice for the mother of the bride to strew salt and dill in her shoes prior to her going to the church, repeating at the same time this charm—

> "Dill, cease not from Will,
> Salt relax not."

It is also customary for both bride and bridegroom to strew dill and salt in their shoes as a charm against every kind of malignant influence.

In the Northern Counties, a bride is expressly warned, "be sure when you go to get married that you don't go in at one door and out at another, or you will be always unlucky." An instance of a similar piece of folk-lore is recorded by the late Cuthbert Bede in *Notes and Queries* as having occurred at a wedding that took place in a Worcestershire village in October, 1877. He thus writes : "The bride and bridegroom at the conclusion of the ceremony left the church by the chancel door, instead of following the usual custom of walking down the church and through the nave door. One of the oldest inhabitants, in mentioning this to me, said that 'it betokened bad luck,' and that she had never known a like instance but once in her life, when the married couple went out of the church through the chancel door, and the bride was a widow before the twelve months were out."

There is, too, a widespread notion that when the bride retires to bed on her wedding night, her bridesmaids should lay her stockings across the bed, as this act is supposed to guarantee her future posterity in the marriage state. It has also long been a popular superstition that the bride should weep on her wedding day—if it be only a few tears—the omission of such an act being considered ominous of all future happiness.

Turning to the bridesmaids, it appears that as far back as the days of the Anglo-Saxons they attended the bride at the wedding ceremony, although in later times they seem to have escorted the bridegroom, his friends waiting on the bride. As recently, for instance, as the last century, this was the popular mode of procedure, an illustration of which is given in the "Collier's Wedding":—

"Two lusty lads, well dressed and strong,
Stept out to lead the bridegroom along;
And two young maids or equal size,
As soon the bridegroom's hands surprise."

Spenser, in his charming picture of an Elizabethan bridal—"The Wedding of the Medway and the

Thames"—gives the bride for her attendants, two bridesmaids, and two bride-pages:—

> "On her two pretty bridesmaids did attend,
> Which on her waited, things amiss to mend,
> And her before there paced pages twain,
> Both clad in colours like, and like away."

Instead of being so many graceful ornaments at the marriage ceremony, as nowadays, the bridesmaids in days of old had various duties assigned to them—one of their principal tasks having been to dress the bride, when any omission in her toilet was laid to their charge. It was the first bridesmaid's duty, too, to see that each of the bridesmaids was not only provided with a sprig of rosemary, or a floral posy, but had a symbolical chaplet in her hand.

A survival of this practice may still be seen in Germany, where it is customary for the bridesmaids to carry the myrtle wreath—which they have subscribed together to purchase on the nuptial-eve—to the house of the bride, and to remove it from her head at the close of the wedding day. After this has been done, the bride is blindfolded, and, the myrtle wreath having been put into her hand, she tries to place it on the head of one of her bridesmaids, as they dance round her, for, in accordance with an old belief, whoever she crowns is sure to be married within a year from that date.

Again, much importance was formerly attached to the colours which the bride wore on her wedding day. In an old book, entitled "The Fifteen Comforts of Marriage," a bride and her bridesmaids are represented conversing together, respecting the colours to be used for the decoration of the bridal dress. It was finally decided, after various colours had been rejected, " to mingle a gold tissue with grass-green," this combination being considered symbolical of youth and jollity.

In Scotland the bridesmaid is popularly known as the " best maid," and, in past years, one of her principal duties was to carry the bride's presents on the wedding day to her future home. The first article generally taken into the house was a vessel of salt, a portion of which was sprinkled over the floor as a protection against the malignant influence of the "Evil Eye." And Mr. W. Gregor, describing an old Scotch wedding, tells us, the bridesmaids' position was not unattended with certain risks : " After the church had been opened, the beadle or bellman was in attendance to lead the bridegroom to the *bride-steel*—that is, the pew that was set apart for the use of those who were to be married. The bride was now led forth and placed beside him, and great care was used to have her placed at the proper side. To have placed her improperly would have been unlucky in the extreme. Next to the bride stood her ' best maid,' this office, though accounted an honour, not being unattended with risk. Three times a bridesmaid was the inevitable prelude of remaining unmarried."

Lastly, it was one of the duties of the bridesmaid to remind the bride of guarding against certain omens, which were supposed to be attended with fatal results. In making a wedding trip, for instance, she was enjoined " to be sure and always go up against the stream, as it was most uncanny to go down the waters."

One of the most interesting antiquities ot Jarrow Church, Northumberland, is the chair of the Venerable Bede, kept in the vestry, whither brides, conducted by their bridesmaids, at once repair, after the marriage service, to seat themselves upon it. According to the general belief, this act will, in due time, make them the joyous mothers of children, and no wedding ceremony is considered complete until the bride has been duly enthroned.

Similarly, in days gone by, on the lower declivity of Warton Crag, in the parish of Warton, Lancashire, a seat, locally known as the " Bride's Chair," was commonly resorted to on their wedding day by the brides of the village, where they were solemnly enthroned.

But, on the other hand, in past years every precaution was taken to prevent a bride sitting down on the left seat at the gateway of the entrance to Great Yarmouth Parish Church—popularly designated the " Devil's Seat," as such an act, it was said, would in days to follow render her specially liable to misfortune.

According to another popular item of folk-lore, " if a horse stood and looked through a gateway, or along a road, where a bride or bridegroom dwelt, it was considered to be a bad omen for that future couple ;" and one most important parting warning to the bride was that she should remember, "whoever goes to sleep first on the wedding night will be the first to die."

Although, therefore, at the present day, the bride's lady attendants are so many pretty and attractive appendages of the nuptial ceremony—symbols, oftentimes of youth and beauty—they were not only formerly far less elaborately dressed, but, as seen in the previous pages, they had duties to perform of a responsible nature, the omission of which was thought to presage unhappiness to the bride.

CHAPTER XXIII

SUPERSTITIONS ABOUT WOMEN

"'Tis a history
Handed from ages down; a nurse's tale,
Which children, open-eyed and mouth'd, devour;
And thus, as garrulous ignorance relates,
We learn it, and believe."

THE life of woman from the cradle to the grave has always, from the earliest period, been surrounded with all manner of curious beliefs, some of which have already been incidentally alluded to in the preceding pages. And, strange to say, even at the present day, these old-world fancies—childish as they only too frequently are—exercise, not unfrequently, a strong influence even in high places upon womankind, and oftentimes they crop up in the most unexpected manner when urged in support of some event in a woman's life—either for weal or woe—which, by the credulous, is held to be the natural outcome of fate as expressed in what may be termed folk-lore formulas.

Thus, to give a few popular illustrations, many a woman has attributed her misfortune in life to having been a "May chet"—that is, born in May; for, as the adage runs:—

> "May chets,
> Bad luck begets;"

whilst, in the West of England, a girl's future is still supposed to be, more or less, determined by the day of her birth, for "Sunday's child is full of grace," and as an old couplet says:—

> "The child of Sunday and Christmas Day
> Is good and fair, and wise and gay."

And, in the same way, popular imagination has gathered from certain features of a woman's person supposed indications not only of her character, but also of events likely, sooner or later, to befall her. A mole on the neck, for instance, denotes that there is wealth in store for her, a local rhyme, often quoted in the county of Nottingham, running thus:—

> "I have a mole above my right eye,
> And shall be a lady before I die;
> As things may happen, as things may fall,
> Who knows but that I may be Lady of Bunny Hall?"

and, according to another version, of which there are several, we are reminded that—

> "If you've got a mole above your chin,
> You'll never be beholden to any of your kin."

Similarly, inferences of various kinds have, at one time or another, been drawn from the eyes, although these have not always been of a very auspicious character, for it said of the eyebrows—

> "They that meet across the nose,
> Will never wear their wedding clothes."

Another version being thus :—

> "If your eyebrows meet across the nose,
> You'll never live to wear your wedding clothes." [1]

But superstitious fancies connected with the eye have existed everywhere, and a piece of Indian folk-lore tells us that—

> "When the right eye throbs, it's mother or sister coming ;
> When the left eye throbs, it's brother or husband coming ;"

an omen which, by the by, is very old, being mentioned by Theocritus, who says : "My right eye issues now, and I shall see my love." And this notion survives to-day, for, according to the popular adage, "When the right eye itches, the party affected will shortly cry ; if the left, they will laugh." And in the old days, when one of the terrors of daily life was the "evil eye"—to which both sexes were thought to be exposed, an allusion to which delusion is made in "Titus Andronicus" (act ii. sc. 1), where Aaron speaks of Timora as—

> ". . . fettered in amorous chains,
> And faster bound to Aaron's charming eyes
> Than is Prometheus tied to Caucasus"—

[1] See further allusions in the Chapter on the Eyes.

the "wise woman" was much in request, her advice in case of emergency having been freely sought to the lucrative profit of her own pocket. Sometimes the woman was the guilty person in the matter of the "evil eye," as appeared from a case brought some years ago before the Guardians of the Shaftesbury Union, in which an appellant for relief stated that he was unable to earn his livelihood through having been "overlooked" by his sister-in-law. It was stated in evidence that, although his wife had resorted for help to a "Wise Woman," it was to no purpose, as her efforts were perfectly ineffectual to remove the spell under which he lay.

Among other indications that some influence, either good or the reverse, is at work, is what is commonly called "cheek burning," and, in case it should be the latter, the following curse has long been repeated at such a time by the fair sex :—

"Right cheek, left cheek, why do you burn ?
Cursed be she that doth me any harm :
If she be a maid, let her be staid ;
If she be a widow, long let her mourn ;
But if it be my own true love—burn, cheek, burn !"

A "blue vein" across the nose has, from time immemorial, been regarded by the fair sex as "a hateful sign," and oftentimes it has been the cause of much needless alarm. Among the many instances given of this folk-lore belief may be quoted one narrative in Hunt's "Popular Romances of the West of England": "A fond mother was paying more than ordinary attention to a fine healthy-looking child, a boy, about three years old. The poor woman's breast was heaving with emotion, and she struggled to repress her sighs. Upon inquiring if anything was really wrong, she said: 'The lady of the house had just told her that the child could not live long, because he had a blue vein across his nose.'"

But just as lucky is the young girl supposed to be whose teeth are wide apart, such a peculiarity being held to be a sure indication of her bright and prosperous future. A correspondent of *Notes and Queries* writes thus: "A young lady, the other day, in reply to an observation of mine, 'What a lucky girl you are,' answered, 'So they used to say I should be, when at school.' 'Why?' 'Because my teeth were set so far apart; it was a sure sign that I should be lucky, and travel.'" Indeed, there is scarcely a part of the human body which has not had some piece of folk-lore attached to it; and Suffolk girls are still in the habit of humming the well-known doggerel when occasion requires:—

"If your head itches
You're going to get riches;
Rub it on wood,
Sure to come good;
Rub it on iron,
Sure to come flying;
Rub it on brass,
Sure to come to pass;
Rub it on steel,
Sure to come a deal;
Rub it on tin,
Sure to come agin."

And, it may be added, with slight variation, this rhyme is used of the right ankle and hand.

There are a good many curious items of folk-lore relating to the growth of the hair; and, according to a Yorkshire belief, when a woman's hair grows in a low point on the forehead, it is commonly supposed to presage widowhood, and is hence nicknamed "a widow's peak." A great deal of hair on the head has, in the case of both sexes, been said to be indicative of a lack of brains, a belief embodied in the familiar proverb, "Bush natural, more hairs than wit." Thus Shakespeare alludes to this popular fancy in the "Two Gentlemen of Verona" (act iii. sc. 2) where he makes Speed say: "She hath more hair than wit, and more faults than brain, and more wealth than faults." It is interesting, again, to note that in German folk-lore the idea of hair as a substitute for its owner is discernible; where a practice known as "hair-snatching" is observed. By this means, on St. Andrew's Day, anxious aspirants to matrimony may ascertain what coloured hair their future husbands have. The mode of procedure is for the young lady towards midnight to take hold of the latch of the door, and to call out three times, "Gentle love, if thou lovest me, show thyself!" She must then open the door a few inches, make a sudden snatch out in the dark, when she will find in her hand a lock of her future husband's hair. One of the indispensable conditions for the success of this charm is that she should be quite alone in the house, and make the trial unknown to any one. The same notion of substitution occurs in the love-charms of this country; and, according to one old formula, "two girls must sit in a room by themselves from twelve o'clock at night till one o'clock in the morning, without speaking. During this time each must take as many hairs from her head as she is years old, and having put them into a linen cloth, with some of the herb *true-love*, as soon as the clock strikes one, she must turn every hair separately, saying—

> "I offer this my sacrifice,
> To him most precious in my eyes;
> I charge thee now come forth to me,
> That I this minute may thee see."

Indeed the anxious maiden, in her natural longings to lift the veil of futurity, has rarely failed to find a sign or token of the kind required, not only in some natural objects, such as birds, animals, insects, moss and plants, but even in such trivial objects as those connected with her own dress. Thus girls when in a strange bed would, in years past, tie their garters nine times round the bed-post, and knit as many knots in them, repeating these lines by way of incantation—

> "This knot I knit, this knot I tie,
> To see my lover as he goes by,
> In his apparel and array,
> As he walks in every day;"

there being various versions of this rhyme, one of which runs thus:—

> "This knot I knit
> To know the thing I know not yet:
> That I may see
> The man that shall my husband be;
> How he goes and what he wears,
> And what he does all days and years."

In the same way, on a Friday night, the young girl would draw her left stocking into her right, saying:—

> "This is the blessed Friday night
> I draw my left stocking into my right;
> To dream of the living, not of the dead,
> To dream of the young man I am to wed."

Many omens have long been drawn by women from the shoe, and according to the teaching of a Suffolk rhyme:—

> "Tip at the toe, live to see woe;
> Wear at the side, live to be a bride;
> Wear at the ball, live to spend all;
> Wear at the back, live to save a deal."

And the time-honoured practice for young girls to place their shoes in the form of the letter T still survives, with its couplet—

> "Hoping this night my true love to see,
> I place my shoes in the form of a T."

But leaving dress, with its many superstitions, we find even the cat the object of superstition, for it is commonly said in the northern counties:

> "Whenever the cat of the house is black,
> The lasses of lovers will have no lack."

And there is the deep-rooted but groundless belief of many a young mother that pussy stiffles the breath of the baby if she gets the chance, and peasant girls in our northern counties, too, still cling to the notion that—

> "Kiss the black cat, an' 'twill make ye fat ;
> Kiss the white one, 'twill make ye lean."

The old belief of placing, as a charm, a knife near a sleeping child has not died out, and what Herrick long ago described is repeated to-day :—

> "Let the superstitious wife
> Near the child's heart lay a knife,
> Point be up, and haft be down ;
> While she gossips in the town.
> This 'mong other mystic charms
> Keeps the sleeping child from harms."

In the midland counties, grandmothers exclaim, "God help you ! " when they hear a child sneeze ; and Scotch folk-lore tells us that a new-born child is considered by its nurse to be in the fairy spells until it has sneezed.

According to a Shropshire belief, it is said that :—

> "She that pricks bread with fork or knife
> Will never be a happy maid or wife ; "

for this little act should always be done with a skewer. A common notion, too, is that if a loaf accidentally part in the hand of an unmarried girl, she will have little or no chance of getting married during the next twelve months ; and the same result is supposed to follow, if at a social gathering a girl is inadvertently placed between a man and his wife.

Imaginary impediments to matrimony of this kind are very numerous in a woman's folk-lore, and it is through the same fear that Swedish young ladies abstain from looking into the glass after dark, or by candlelight, for fear of forfeiting the good opinion of the opposite sex. Similarly, in this and other countries, there is a strong antipathy among the fair sex for one to even look at a man, however attractive he may be, whose name commences with the same letter as her own ; for, in marriage—

> "To change the name and not the letter,
> Is a change for the worse and not the better."

And we may note here that among the many reasons assigned for the ill-luck of May marriages is that not only from such union, "All the bairns die and decay," but that women disobeying the rule would be childless ; or, if they had children, that the first-born would be an idiot, or have some physical deformity ; or that the married couple would not live happily in their new life, but in a very short time grow weary of each other's society—popular fancies which are still held by women.

Strange to say, a somewhat similar penalty is said, in the North of England, to overtake the rash young lady who is present at church when the banns of marriage are put up, as any children she may hereafter have run the risk of being born deaf and dumb. The same notion prevails in Worcestershire, and some years ago a correspondent of *Notes and Queries* tells how a girl urged as an excuse for not hearing the publication of her banns the risk of bringing the curse of dumbness on her offspring, adding that one of her friends who had transgressed this rule "by hearing herself asked out at church," in due course had six children, all of whom were deaf and dumb.

Omens from dreams have, at all times, held a prominent place in a woman's folk-lore, and one may often hear a Shropshire damsel use the proverbial old couplet which tells how—

> "A Friday night's dream on Saturday told,
> Is due to come true be it never so old";

which is much after the same fashion as a couplet current in Gloucestershire :—

> "Friday night's dream mark well,
> Saturday night's dream ne'er tell."

Indeed, Friday's dreams would seem to be regarded by women with special favour, in illustration of which belief may be quoted a rhyme current in Norfolk :—

> "To-night, to-night, is Friday night,
> Lay me down in dirty white,
> Dream whom my husband is to be;
> And lay my children by my side,
> If I'm to live to be his bride."

The interpretation of dreams has, in most countries, been made the subiect of much ingenious speculation, and many a "Dictionary of Dreams" has been framed to help the fair sex in this matter. But, of the thousand and one incidents which are ever nightly being repeated in dreamland, there would seem to be a consensus of opinion in dream books that dreaming of balls and dancing indicates some stroke of good luck in the marriage way to the young lady, it being said that those

> "Who dream of being at a ball
> No cause have they for fear,
> For soon will they united be
> To those they hold most dear."

And a further example we may quote from "Mother Bunch's Closet Newly Broke Open" (Percy Society, xxiii. 10–11), because this mode of divination has been one, perhaps more than any other, practised both at home and abroad by young girls anxious to gain a sweetheart :—

"Yet I have another pretty way for a maid to know her sweetheart, which is as follows : Take a summer apple of the best fruit, stick pins close into the apple to the head, and as you stick them, take notice which of them is the middlemost, and give it what name you fancy, put it into thy left-hand glove, and lay it under thy pillow on Saturday night when thou gettest into bed, then clap thy hands together, and say these words :—

> "'If thou be he that must have me
> To be thy wedded bride,
> Make no delay but come away,
> This night to my bedside.'"

CHAPTER XXIV

WOMAN'S TEARS

"Tears are the strength of women."—SAINT EVREMOND.

THE propensity for a woman to shed tears on the slightest emotion has long been the subject of frequent comment in proverbial literature, and, according to Ricard, "Women never weep more bitterly than when they weep with spite." This common occurrence of everyday life is thus noticed in a popular Scotch adage, which tells us that "It's nae mair ferlie to see a woman greet than to see a guse gang barefit"—the meaning being that it is no more wonder to see a woman cry than to see a goose "go barefoot." Indeed, this characteristic of woman, it might be expected, has not escaped ridicule and censure, for, according to an old Latin proverb, "The laughter, the tears, and the song of a woman are equally deceptive;" which is somewhat after the same fashion as the French maxim, "A woman's tears are a fountain of craft;" and the Spanish proverb, "A woman's tears and a dog's limping are not real." How little is required to make a woman weep has been noticed by Sir Walter Scott, who pictured aright human life when he wrote :—

> "A child will weep at a bramble's smart,
> A maid to see her sparrow part,
> A stripling for a woman's heart ;
> But woe awaits a country when
> She sees the tears of bearded men."

And, among the many proverbial maxims which endorse this view, we may quote this couplet :—

> "Deceit, weeping, spinning, God hath give
> To women, kindly, while they may live."

Much to the same purport is the Italian adage :—

> "A woman complains, a woman's in woe ;
> A woman is sick when she likes to be so ;"

and the old French saying, which says, "Women laugh when they can and weep when they will." But, as Joanna Baillie, in "Basil," truly writes :—

> "Woman's grief is like a summer storm,
> Short as it is violent"—

a statement borne out by the popular saying, which likens her tears to an April shower, which is generally sharp and soon over.

But, given as a woman is to tears, grief would not seem to injure her, if there be any truth in the proverb which says, "A cat has nine lives, and a woman has nine cats' lives," an allusion to which quaint belief occurs in Middleton's "Blurt, Master Constable," 1602, where we find this passage: "They have nine lives apiece, like a woman;" and the same idea is conveyed in the proverb, quoted elsewhere, "Though most women be long-lived, yet they all die with an ill-will."

It is generally supposed that a woman who laughs before breakfast will cry before night, with which agrees the Scotch proverb, "Laugh at leisure; ye may greet ere night."

In the evidence given at an inquest on the bodies of four persons killed by an explosion at a firework manufactory in Bermondsey, October 12, 1849, one of the witnesses stated: "On Friday they were all very merry, and Mrs. B—— said she feared something would happen before they went to bed, because they were so happy."

But even a woman's smiles must be received with caution, it is said, come when they may, for, as the Italians say, "The smiles of a pretty woman are the tears of the purse;" or, as another version has it, "When a pretty woman laughs it is certain that a purse complains."

CHAPTER XXV

WOMAN'S BLUSHES

"From every blush that kindles in thy cheeks
Ten thousand little loves and graces spring,
To revel in the roses."—ROWE, *Tamerlane.*

PERHAPS one of the most charming characteristics of maidenhood is its transient blush, which poets with all their wealth of poetic imagery have depicted in a thousand pretty ways, so often described by them as playing on the cheeks with all the roseate hue of loveliness, and what more graceful picture can there be than Gay has given us :—

"The rising blushes which her cheek o'erspread,
Are opening roses in the lily's bed."

Such Shakesperian expressions as "Bid the cheek be ready with a blush, modest as morning," "Thy cheeks blush with pure shame to counterfeit our roses," and "To blush and beautify the cheek again," would seem to suggest the high charm blushes had for Shakespeare; although, on the other hand, expressions like the following must be held to imply a very different meaning—"Her blush is gluttiness, not modesty," and "Blushing cheeks by faults are bred, and fears by pale white shown." But, however numerous the diverse views of this kind may be—many of which have been embodied in proverbial literature—there can be no doubt that the consensus of opinion, both at home and abroad, has always been in favour of a woman's blush, for, in accordance with the time-honoured adage, "Blushing is virtue's colour."

Even the Circassian women who are capable ot blushing fetch a higher price in the seraglio of the Sultan than less susceptible women; and Darwin quotes from Humboldt an adage of the Spaniard, "How can those be trusted who know not how to blush?"

Indeed, it has been observed, she who has lost the art of blushing has lost the most powerful charm of beauty, for deprived of her most maidenly blushes what would Parnell's beauty have been:—

> "A crimson blush her beauteous face o'erspread,
> Varying her cheeks, by turn, with white and red;
> The driving colours, never at a stay,
> Run here and there, and flush, and fade away."

But the Italians have a proverb, which is often applied to those who mar their features by artificial colouring, "Women rouge that they may not blush." As might be expected, all kinds of strange views have at one time or another been held in most countries respecting blushing, some of the explanations not always being very complimentary to the fair sex. Thus, according to one popular fancy, it is supposed to be an indication of conscious deceit, and in the "Passionate Pilgrim," we find this allusion to blushing, which under one form or another has been variously expressed :—

"Yet will she blush, here be it said,
To hear her secrets so betrayed."

Pope writes, "Do good by stealth, and blush to find it fame;" but George Eliot, in "Daniel Deronda,"[1] speaks somewhat disparagingly of the blush, which she says "is no language; only a dubious flag-signal, which may mean either of two contradictions;" and Moore speaks of—

"Playful blushes that seem nought
But luminous escapes of thought."

It has long been a much disputed question—and one which does not seem altogether to have been satisfactorily answered—as to whether blushing takes place in the dark, an interesting correspondence relative to which was carried on a few years back in the pages of *Notes and Queries*,[2] when Mr. J. C. Galton expressed his opinion in the negative.

[1] Book v., chap. xxxv.
[2] See *Notes and Queries*, 5th Series, vii. p. 145.

Darwin, however, appears to have thought differently, for, in his "Expressions of the Emotions," he thus alludes to this subject:—

"The fact that blushes may be excited in absolute solitude seems opposed to the view, namely, that the habit originally arose from thinking about what others think of us. Several ladies who are great blushers, are unanimous in regard to solitude, and some of them believe that they have blushed in the dark. From what Mr. Forbes has stated with regard to the Aymaras, and from my own sensations, I have no doubt that this latter statement is correct. Shakespeare, therefore, erred when he made Juliet, who was not even by herself, say to Romeo (act ii. sc. 2):—

"'Thou know'st the mark of night is on my face;
Else would a maiden's blush bedeck my cheek,
For that which thou hast heard me speak to-night.'"

CHAPTER XXVI

DAUGHTERS

"My son is my son till he hath got him a wife,
But my daughter's my daughter all the days of her life."

THE proper bringing up, and putting out in life, of daughters have always been a moot point in proverbial philosophy, but it would seem that most countries are agreed in regarding marriage as the best thing for their happiness, although this is not always an easy matter, for, as it is said in Germany, "Daughters are easy to rear, but difficult to marry;" which is much to the same purport as the Spanish adage, "When a good offer comes for a daughter, don't wait till her father returns from market," for fear the opportunity should slip by; another German saying reminding us that "Daughters and dead fish are no keeping wares." There are numerous versions of this piece of proverbial philosophy, a well-known adage recommending parents thus: "Marry your son when you will, your daughter when you can."

It is not every parent, it may be remembered, who is in the position to make conditions similar to the following, told in a West African folk-tale :—

A certain man had a most beautiful daughter, who was beset by many suitors. But as soon as they were told that the sole condition on which they could obtain her was to bale out a brook with a ground nut shell they always walked away in disappointment. However, at last one took heart of grace and began the task. He obtained the young lady, for the father said, "He who undertakes what he says, will do it."

À propos of the value of grown-up daughters, an amusing story is told by Mr. Baring Gould in illustration of a curious baptismal superstition which still lingers on in Yorkshire, where it is said the first child baptised in a new font is sure to die—a reminiscence of the sacrifice which was used for the consecration of every dwelling and temple in heathen times.

"When I was incumbent of Dalton," he writes, "a new church was built. A blacksmith in the village had seven daughters, after which a son was born, and he came to me a few days after the consecration of the new church to ask me to baptise his boy in the old temporary church and font.

"'Why, Joseph,' said I, 'if you only wait till Thursday, the boy can be baptised in the new font on the opening of the new church.'

"'Thank you, sir,' replied the blacksmith with a wriggle, 'but, you see, it's a lad, and we shu'd be sorry if he were to die; ha' if t'had been a lass instead, why then, you were welcome, for 'twouldn't ha' mattered a ha'penny. Lasses are ower money, and lads ower few wi' us.' "

But the blacksmith's reference to his seven daughters reminds us that for very many years past extraordinary powers have been generally supposed to reside in the "seventh daughter," strange instances of which have from time to time been recorded in the literature of the past. Thus the Scotch fortune-teller commonly boasted that she was the seventh daughter of a seventh daughter, and by this means she contrived to ingratiate herself among the lower orders.

A correspondent of *Notes and Queries*, writing some years ago, records how "In Saltash Street, Plymouth, my friend copied on December 10, 1852, the following notice on a board, indicating the profession and claims of the inhabitant: 'A. Shepherd, the third seventh daughter—doctress.' " As in the case of the "seventh son," such a child is born a physician, possessing an intuitive knowledge of the art of healing all manners of disorders, and even occasionally the faculty of performing wonderful cures by only the touch of the finger. Some years ago a herbalist in the West of England declared that she was "in the habit of healing scores of people that medical men had given up," her credentials being that she was the seventh daughter of the seventh daughter of the seventh daughter.

And to this day, in some places, there exists a strong prejudice against baptising a boy before a girl, an amusing instance of which is given by the late Cuthbert Bede in *Notes and Queries* as having occurred in a Worcestershire parish.

On the occasion in question there were three baptisms, two boys and a girl, and when the first child was about to be christened the woman who carried the little girl elbowed her way up to the parson, in order that the child in her arms might be the first to be baptized. By way of apology, she said to one of the sponsors, "It's a girl, so it must be christened first."

On the following day an opportunity was taken to ascertain her motive, and this was her explanation: "You see, sir, the parson bain't a married man, and consequentially is disfamiliar with children, or he'd a-never put the little girl to be christened after the boys. And although it sadly fluster'd me, sir, to put myself afore my betters in the way which I was fosed to do, yet, sir, it was the doing of a kindness to them two little boys in me a-setting of my little daughter afore 'em."

"Why?"

"Well, sir, if them little boys had been christened afore the little girl, they'd have her soft chin and she'd have had their hairy beards—the poor little incident! But, thank goodness, I've kept her from that misfortune."

On the other hand, strange to say, in Scotland, and in some parts of the North of England, just the reverse practice is observed, the Scotch reason being that to christen a girl before a boy would be to make the former of a masculine nature, while the latter would grow up effeminate. A correspondent of *Notes and Queries*, writing from Darlington in 1867, says, "While standing at the font, and preparing to baptise two children, the nurse attending on one of the parties abruptly demanded of the other nurse if the child she presented was a boy. When questioned on the subject, she replied that 'she wondered at my not knowing that a boy was always christened before a girl.'"

An amusing equivocal rhyme long current in Durham tells how—

"John Lively, Vicar of Kelloe,
Had seven daughters and never a fellow,"

which, it has been suggested, "may either mean that the parson of the sixteenth century had no son, or that he had no equal in learning." Another version of the proverb reads "six daughters"—seven, it is said, being often merely a conventional number. But, whatever the object of this folk-rhyme may be, the parson mentions no son in his will, in which he leaves to his daughter Elisabeth his best gold ring with a death's head in it, and seventeen yards of white cloth for curtains of a bed, and to his daughter Mary his silver seal of arms, his gimald ring, and black gold ring.[1]

Grown-up daughters at home would occasionally seem to have been regarded the opposite of a blessing to their father, for "Three daughters and

[1] See Halliwell's "Popular Rhymes," 1849, p. 202, and Hazlitt's "English Proverbs," 1869, p. 250.

a mother," runs the German proverb, "are four devils for the father;" but, it is added, "Would you know your daughter, see her in company," for then she will cultivate every charm to make herself as attractive as possible. At home the picture is quite the reverse, for, runs the popular German adage, "A house full of daughters is like a cellar full of sour beer;" and there is our own proverb, "Marriageable, foolish wenches are troublesome troops to keep."

A Cheshire maxim, too, speaks in the same strain:—

> "I'll tent thee, quoth Wood,
> If I can't rule my daughter, I'll rule my good."

This idea, it may be added, is conveyed in various ways, which, it must be acknowledged, are far from being favourable to the children, for, as a Northamptonshire couplet says:—

> "As tall as your knee they are pretty to see;
> As tall as your head they wish you were dead."

Hence daughters are certain cares, but uncertain comforts; and, according to an Oriental proverbial maxim—

> "A daughter after two sons brings prosperity,
> And a son after two daughters beggary."

And we may compare the Lincolnshire couplet—

> "Lasses is cumbersome,
> Lads is lumbersome."

Folk-maxims of this kind might be easily multiplied, a popular Welsh adage reminding us that "the worst store is a maid unbestowed," but when it is remembered in the words of our old proverb that "Every Jack must have his Jill," there is hope for every daughter of Eve, for she may be the object of a passion similar to that described by Charles Dance :—

"By the margins of fair Zurich's waters
 Dwelt a youth, whose fond heart, night and day,
For the fairest of fair Zurich's daughters,
 In a dream of love melted way."

CHAPTER XXVII

MY LADY'S WALK

"Lady of the mere
Sole-sitting by the shores of old romance."
WORDSWORTH.

ASSOCIATED with many of our historic houses and romantic spots, "My Lady's Walk" perpetuates the memory, not infrequently, of traditions of a tragic and legendary kind, some of which belong to incidents bound up with the seamy side of family romance.

Thus at Huddington, Worcestershire, there is an avenue of trees called "Lady Winter's Walk," where, it is said, the lady of Thomas Winter—who was forced to conceal himself on account of his share in the Gunpowder Plot—was in the habit of awaiting her husband's furtive visits; and here, it is affirmed, her ladyship is still occasionally seen pacing up and down her old accustomed haunt beneath the sombre shade of those aged trees.

Near Guy's Cave, Warwick, there is "Fair Phillis's Walk," where, according to the local tradition, she was in the habit of daily sauntering, lamenting the absence of her husband Guy, whom she supposed to be dead, or a prisoner in the Holy Land, while, all the time, he was in close proximity to her, living in a cave, disguised as a palmer, which, runs the story, was constructed by himself, for—

> "There, with my hands, I hewed a house,
> Out of a craggy rock of stone,
> And lived like a palmer poor,
> Within that cave myself alone."

It appears that he was obliged to betake himself to this life of penance from remorse at having wrought so much mischief for the sake of the fair Phillis, who, after the fashion of the noble ladies of her time, required deeds of arms from her lover before she would acknowledge his attentions. But he made himself known to her when dying, and ever since this romantic episode the spot in question has been known as "Fair Phillis's Walk."

A deep ravine within the summit of Walla Crag, Keswick, "in whose ponderous jaws," tradition says, "the once errant spirit of Jamie Lowther—the first Earl of Lonsdale—was securely immured, is still known as the "Lady's Rake," being the path by which, according to an improbable story, the Countess of Derwentwater effected her escape on receiving the news of her husband's capture, carrying with her a quantity of jewels and other valuables. She fled, it is said, along this memorable path "from the rage of the peasantry, who considered her to be the cause of the earl's misfortune, having instigated him to take part in the rebellion against his better judgment."

Similarly, the Ermine Street, running from Godmanchester towards Stamford and Lincoln, was in years past locally designated "Lady Coneyborough's Way," from an old tradition, long remembered in the neighbourhood, that, when St. Kneyburgh was once pursued by a ruffianly assailant, "the road unrolled itself before her as she fled," and thus enabled her to effect her escape in safety.

About two miles from Bolton Castle, on the ridge of Leyburn Shawl—a green terrace about a mile long—there is a narrow way, or pass, which is commonly known as the "Queen's Gap." At this spot, the story goes, Mary Queen of Scots was caught by Lord Scrope and his guards, when attempting to make her escape from Bolton Castle. The pass since that day—as the place of her recapture—has invariably, it is said, been known as the "Queen's Gap"; but such an attempt was probably never made, although, as it has been added, "the Shawl must have been visited by the Queen, who, whilst at Bolton, was allowed to ride forth hunting and hawking," under due supervision.

Historic romance affords numerous examples of walks rendered famous by the fair sex under a variety of peculiar circumstances. According to a village tradition current at Ludgershall, Buckinghamshire, this locality was selected by Henry II. as a retreat for fair Rosamond, whose memory is still perpetuated by a lane in the woods popularly called "Rosamond's Way." Again, within a short distance of Brougham Castle stands the "Countess Pillar," the approach to which has a romantic interest from having been traversed by two celebrated ladies. The pillar was erected in the year 1656 by Lady Anne Clifford—"a memorial," as its inscription informs us, "of her last parting at that place with her good and pious mother, Margaret Countess Dowager of Cumberland, on the 2nd of April, an eventful incident which has thus been poetically described:—

> "That modest stone by pious Pembroke rear'd,
> Which still recalls beyond the pencil's power
> The silent sorrows of a parting hour."

Mab's Cross, again, which stands at the top of Standish Gate, Wigan, at the entrance of the town, commemorates the story of Lady Mabel Bradshaigh, who, during her husband's absence of ten years in the Holy Wars, married a Welsh knight. On his return Sir William Bradshaigh was outlawed "for a year and a day for killing the Welsh Knight," and Lady Mabel was enjoined to do penance "by going once every week barefooted" to the aforesaid Cross, the lane along which she went from Haigh Hall having been known as Mab's Lane.

But a more pleasing memory is attached to Newark Castle, which was the early home of the

Duchess of Monmouth and Buccleuch, and the scene of Sir Walter Scott's "Lay of the Last Minstrel," which he recited for amusement. Amidst the many historic associations connected with this locality, a walk leading from Bowhill by the Yarrow to the old Castle is called the "Duchess's Walk," thereby perpetuating the traditions of the past. And it may be remembered how in the old days of the Scotch Court, when tournaments and other chivalrous sports were in fashion at Stirling, it was customary for the ladies of the Court to assemble on what is still denominated the "Ladies' Rock" to "survey the knightly feats of their admirers." It was here that a tournament was held in the year 1506, in honour of a blackamoor girl, who had been captured in a Portugese ship, the jousting on this occasion being conducted with unusual splendour.

Among the numerous historical episodes and domestic incidents associated with Haddon Hall, tradition still delights to preserve the romance attached to the fine avenue called "Dorothy's Walk," for it was from "Dorothy Vernon's Door," with its overhanging ivy and sycamore, that the beautiful heiress of Haddon stole out one night, like Jessica, to join her lover, the spot in the terrace, known to this day as "the Ladies' Steps," being where the meeting took place. The elopement of Dorothy Vernon has employed the pen of the novelist and the poet, and it has been thrown into the form of a story, "The Love Steps of Dorothy Vernon."

On the other hand, a Welsh tradition points

out "the Virgin's Meadow," near Dolforwyn Hall, as the romantic scene of the death of "Sabrina fair," whose fate has been the theme of many poets, including Milton and Drayton :—

> "Rocky Dolforwyn,
> Sabrina's early haunt, ere yet she fled
> In search of Gwendolen, her stepdame proud,
> With envious hate enraged."

Under one form or another my so-called "Lady's Walk" has formed the source of much traditionary lore, and in numerous cases it has gained this distinction from its having been the "trysting-place" where, as family history informs us, many a love affair like that of Dorothy Vernon has been secretly arranged. Among the traditions told of Furness Abbey, one of this kind is known as the "Abbey Vows," and records how the pretty squire's daughter repaired to the ruins of Furness Abbey with her lover, ere he went to sea, to pledge their troth. Daily afterwards she regularly went to the Abbey by the same walk to gaze on the spot where they had knelt, and nowadays, although many a year has gone by, "my Lady's Walk" to Furness Abbey is still a household tale.

Lastly, occasionally a more melancholy reason is given for "my Lady's Walk," as is the case of a tradition told in connection with the Spindleston Hills, which are commonly said to be haunted by a lady nicknamed "The Wandering Shepherdess." The story goes that a certain lady, after the death of her lover, abandoned rank and wealth, and spent her remaining days following sheep on the hills, and even now the peasants affirm she may at times be seen doing the same walk, reminding us of the lady with her lantern, who in stormy weather walks up and down the beach at St. Ives on the Cornish coast.

INDEX